D0551573

Y

Mummy's Witness

Mummy's Witness

Gayle Sanders

HODDER &
STOUGHTON

Author's note: Names have been
changed to protect identities, throughout.

Copyright © 2007 by Gayle Sanders

First published in Great Britain in 2007 by Hodder & Stoughton
A division of Hodder Headline

The right of Gayle Sanders to be identified as the Author
of the Work has been asserted by her in accordance
with the Copyright, Designs and Patents Act 1988.

A Hodder & Stoughton Book

1

A CIP catalogue record for this title is available from the British Library

Hardback ISBN 9 78 0 340 93349 7
Trade paperback ISBN 9 78 0 340 95135 4

Typeset in Sabon by Hewer Text UK Ltd, Edinburgh

Printed and bound by Clays Ltd. St Ives plc

Hodder Headline's policy is to use papers that are natural, renewable
and recyclable products and made from wood grown in sustainable forests.
The logging and manufacturing processes are expected to conform
to the environmental regulations of the country of origin.

Hodder & Stoughton Ltd
A division of Hodder Headline
338 Euston Road
London NW1 3BH

For Susan – My Mum

Acknowledgements

In no particular order . . .

I would like to thank all of my wonderful friends and the families who have supported me. Your friendship and support has been both inspiring and encouraging to me over the years. A special and warm-hearted thank you to you all.

Thank you to Stuart for your overwhelming support, compassion and patience. You believed in me when I did not believe in myself.

To the whole team at Hodder, thank you for making this book possible.

Lastly, thank you to my favourite person in the world, Hugh – my husband. Thank you for being you . . .

Contents

Contents

INTRODUCTION

I have written this book for my Mum – Susan. Whilst towards the end of her life she found the courage and strength to challenge my father, she suffered, for most of her married years, in silence. A silence which I now choose to break for her.

It is important to me that those who hear her story understand that my mother did not choose to stay with this man who treated her so cruelly. It was rather that she feared for her life if she tried to leave. And her fears were so tragically confirmed, when she was killed at the point when she was finally breaking free from him.

Research proves that one of the times when a woman is most at risk of being killed by a partner is when she is leaving the relationship. My Mum's death proved this sad statistic all too true.

A mother's love is one of the most precious and vital things in life, and the relationship between mother and child is very special. But, for the bond to flourish, there must be security and confidence. Tragically for my mother and me, my father cruelly interfered with and manipulated our relationship, so that it was impossible for us to develop a real bond. He deliberately prevented us from having the relationship we should have had. This is something I look back upon with deep sadness and regret. I felt helpless and unable to prevent his manipulation and I can only guess that my mother felt the same.

Although I was a child and my father was a big man, my guilt at not being able to challenge or stop him from tormenting my mother – and ultimately from killing her – has never left me. I wish so strongly that my mother had survived. It is a deep pain that refuses to diminish – even with time. That is why, on her behalf, I want to ensure that her silence is broken and that her memory is kept alive.

Whilst my primary motivation for writing this book is to do justice to the memory of my Mum, I have other reasons too. Having worked as a professional in the field of domestic violence I am only too well aware of the myths and stereotypes surrounding it. One of the myths is that it only happens among the poorly educated and worst-off in society. But domestic violence is a classless crime, and my family circumstances highlight this. An apparently nice-looking respectable middle-class family is just as likely to be suffering as any other, and is even more likely to keep it hidden. Just because things appear to be 'normal', it doesn't mean that there aren't problems behind the scenes. Crimes like domestic violence, child abuse and rape all take place in private, and can be kept from public knowledge. Our family troubles, like those of thousands of other families, went on without anyone else ever knowing.

There is another common myth that says alcohol is often involved in domestic violence. But my father never drank – in fact, he believed alcohol to be evil. People choose to behave the way they do regardless of whether they have consumed alcohol.

I want to challenge these myths, and to draw attention to the true facts. I believe that domestic violence and child abuse are crimes which go on silently, in secrecy, among all sections of society, and which deserve more attention and understanding from the public.

My final reason for writing this book is to help, support and inform others, whether they be professionals, victims, survivors, friends or simply those who are interested. I want to highlight the devastating effects of domestic violence and death, especially on the children who are forced to cope with the legacy. A child like me, who witnesses the killing of one parent by the other, is left not only with a broken childhood, but without parents or a home, as well as with the unforgettable images of what they have witnessed. Added to this is the outside world's inability to cope with or help such a traumatised child after the event.

My childhood was one long nightmare which culminated in my mother's death. Afterwards, the love, warmth and security of caring and compassionate, informed adults might have helped me to come to terms with the horrors

I had witnessed. But no one felt able to cope or wanted to know, and the cruelty and brutality that I had suffered at my father's hands were simply swapped for the indifference and neglect of everyone around me, including members of my family. As a result I was sent from one unhappy placement or institution to another. And I remained traumatised and in deep shock for years, unable to grieve for my mother or to feel anything other than desperation and hopelessness. I felt so unlovable that it took me many years and a great deal of painstaking effort before I was able to allow anyone to come close to me, or to find love.

It is important to me to do whatever I can to help prevent another child suffering as I did. My hope is that this book will help to open up a greater debate about domestic violence, and add to the understanding and support of all its victims.

OPENING

As I walked out through the Register Office doors and onto the sweeping front steps, hand in hand with my new husband, I knew that, at last, my time to be happy had come.

Part of me couldn't believe that I was standing there, in my wedding dress, looking out at the laughing faces of so many special friends and beside the man I knew I wanted to be with for the rest of my life.

So many important and loved people were there. The friends I had come to know over the years, whose kindness and warmth I valued so much. Old friends who had supported me through the hardest of times, and my new family; my parents-in-law and sister-in-law who had become so important to me and had done so much to make this a perfect day. And, of course, my oldest friend, Louise, who had known me since we began infant school together when we were five.

As for Hugh, my husband, I felt lucky to have met such

a wonderful man. His warmth, understanding, loyalty and support meant the world to me. I adored him and I knew this was the start of a very happy future. Six months earlier he had proposed, with a bottle of champagne at the ready, as we sat beside the river close to our home, on a warm summer day. I didn't hesitate to say yes: I knew we were right for one another.

Since then we'd had a whirlwind of preparations, plans and endless shopping trips as we organised our wedding. Now here we were, Hugh looking gorgeous in his tails and white tie, me feeling so special in my silk dress and tiara, and around us our four adorable bridesmaids and all the people we cared most about.

As we ducked the clouds of confetti being thrown at us and got into the car taking us to our reception, Hugh smiled and hugged me. Our wedding ceremony had been all that we'd both hoped for. Hugh's father, who was everything a father should be, had given me away, and as he walked me up the aisle I had looked at Hugh and thought: 'This is it – our wedding, the beginning of our life together.'

At the reception, where the room was decorated with white flowers and green berries, we drank champagne, danced and cut our cake. Hugh's father gave a warm speech, and then Louise got to her feet. I had asked her to speak because she, more than anyone, knew how far I had come. It seemed almost a lifetime away from when I had been a little girl of twelve, traumatised and so desperately unhappy that I had wanted to die, rejected by my own family and believing I had no future and was unloved and unwanted by anyone.

Louise had been nervous about giving the speech, but I knew she would get it just right. And she did. She talked about what we'd been like as little girls and how we'd played together, and then she said: 'I know there is one person Gayle misses every single day and who she would love to be here with us now.'

She was right.

My mother.

I wish she had been there, to see me marry the man I loved. To see how I've overcome the tragedy and hurt of the past to build and shape my life and make it a good one, with a happy relationship, a great job and wonderful friends.

It's been a long journey through the twenty years since I lost her. There were many times when I wished I had died too. When I couldn't see a reason for going on, and when I believed that nothing good would ever happen to me again.

I was wrong about that – truly good things have happened.

I hope Mum would be proud of me.

I

Nightmare with no end

Curled into a tight little ball I stayed as still as I could. Barely daring to breathe, I peered out from my hiding place behind a floor-length curtain in the living room. Under the crack at the bottom I could see my mother, who was ironing.

My father had come into the room and was talking to her in a loud, angry voice. Neither of them knew that I was there; I was used to hiding, to staying as still as a little mouse, watching, waiting, every part of me tense with fear.

My father's voice grew louder. He was saying cruel, nasty things to my mother. She had stopped ironing and was beginning to back away as he came closer, shouting his angry, hurtful words in her face, his voice big and powerful.

He started hitting her. She stumbled backwards, and stumbled again as he pushed and shoved her. At the same time he kept telling her how mad and crazy and stupid she was. I could hear her breathing, heavy and fast, not crying but on the verge of crying. Then my father punched her hard and she fell. He turned and left, slamming the door behind him. My mother got to her knees. By this time tears were streaming down her face. After a few minutes she calmed down, got to her feet and called for me.

I wanted to go to her, but I couldn't respond. My throat was too dry to call out, and my body felt paralysed. I knew that she was searching for me, but I was simply unable to move. She went to ask my brother and sister to join in the hunt and eventually one of them found me. My mother said, 'Oh, there you are, thank goodness for that.' She didn't make a big fuss of me, but went to get on with the ironing. I think she probably hoped – and wanted to believe – that I hadn't seen what had happened.

I was just four years old, but scenes like the one I had witnessed seemed like an everyday event in our house. My father attacked my mother, physically and verbally, often with no warning, all the time. His attacks on her were vicious and cruel. He would hurt and belittle her with words and then hit, punch and kick her, twist her arms, throttle her and sit on her.

My mother was an average-sized woman, five feet five inches tall at most, and in those days she was slim, while my father was a big man, well over six feet tall and solidly built, so that he towered over her. He was muscular and powerful and could quite easily knock her across a room.

After each attack he would storm off and my mother would lie on the floor, or on her bed if she could make it that far, crying quietly. Sometimes she would be so badly hurt that she couldn't get out of bed for hours.

He hit me too, often and without warning. I never knew when he might decide I'd got something wrong, or just feel like lashing out. But he saved the worst for Mum, and watching him batter and torment her was much worse than being hit myself.

I had to watch, unable to help her, time and time again, as he tortured and humiliated her, leaving her weeping and in agony. I was desperate to stop him, but I couldn't. My fear paralysed me, and in any case I knew that if I tried he would simply toss me aside. But I still felt that somehow what was happening was my fault.

Ours was a house in which there was no happy family life. Although we did many of the things that other families did, I have no happy memories of my early childhood because fear and anxiety dominated my every waking moment. Even when things appeared relatively normal, I couldn't relax or feel any pleasure, because I knew it wouldn't last.

I spent many hours curled into a ball behind a curtain or a chair, waiting and watching. A lot of the time my parents didn't seem to remember that I existed, so I was able to hide for long periods of time.

From the outside no one would have known that anything was wrong. We lived in Hythe, a small town in Kent, and our modest three-bedroom semi was like any other in the street, with its small front drive and a pleasant garden which backed onto the canal.

My father was a respected local figure and the house came with his job – he taught in a boarding school for children with emotional difficulties. My mother was a housewife, and I had a sister, Sarah, who was seven years older than me, and a brother, John, who was five years older.

We were well behaved, hard-working, respectable and middle-class. Our front garden was neatly trimmed, our car sat in the drive, our school uniforms were clean and ironed and we came and went just like any other family. In fact, in public my father would put on a show of family unity, sitting me on his shoulders and making sure that we appeared like a happy, loving family.

If anything made our family noticeable it was my father's standing in the community. He was a well-known, well-liked man. He knew a huge number of people, particularly among the teaching staff in local schools, and he was known to be a conscientious man who cared a great deal about his job and the children he taught. He was confident, friendly and always willing to stop for a chat or an offer of help. He knew everyone from the local vicar to the milkman and they all liked him.

Because he was a PE teacher he could go to work in tracksuits – he wore them for most of the time, unless he had to be smart for something, in which case he wore cords and a shirt. His style was casual friendly, and this added to the approachable, easygoing image he liked to present to the world. People used to think he was great because he wasn't stuffy and formal.

My mother was much less outgoing. This was probably because of what she was enduring at home, but to other people she was simply a quiet, even shy woman. She stayed at home most of the time and didn't have many friends. When she did go out she always looked well presented, dressing in sensible skirts and with her hair and make-up carefully done. But although if she saw someone she knew she would stop and say hello, it was never for long and she slipped back into the house as soon as her errands were over.

Although we went out and about, no one ever came into our house. The show of normality was put on for the world outside, but behind our front door it was quite a different matter. No family or friends ever came round for a visit or a meal.

I was desperately lonely because I lived without any strong emotional link to another person. My much older brother and sister were like ghosts, sometimes glimpsed but usually somewhere else. Sarah spent a lot of time outside the house. John was quiet and withdrawn and did his best to stay out of everyone's way. So I felt like an only child – a child who, much of the time, was barely noticed by either parent.

On those rare occasions when someone *did* call at our

house, my father was jovial, my mother was polite and we children were quiet. An outsider might have picked up on the tension and felt a little uncomfortable, or noticed that our house was not the warm, cheerful, noisy place that you might expect a family with three children to live in. There were no casually dropped schoolbags, no cosy fires in the hearth, no after-school teas on the table. Instead it was cold, silent and felt almost unlived-in. Everything was clean and in its place, but no care or love had gone into arranging it. There was nothing nice or pretty, and no cosiness or colour.

But while this might have struck a visitor as a little odd they would never have guessed that this was a house where unimaginable violence and cruelty could erupt at any moment, a place ruled over by my father with his unpredictable and monstrous behaviour. Instead, my father would ooze charm and the visitor would leave blinded by his pleasant and concerned manner.

The truth, so carefully hidden from the world, was that ours was a family held together not by love but by fear.

It was seldom anything obvious that provoked my father. Nothing that any of us did or said that would set him off and nothing that my mother could anticipate in any way. So there was absolutely no possibility of avoiding or heading off an attack. He did it because he felt like it. Sometimes I could tell when an assault was imminent because I could see his eyes turn red. When that happened I knew what was coming. But at other times, there was no warning and no way to tell that he was about to strike. His mood would change suddenly and if I was his target the first I would know of it was when he would suddenly get up, stride over to me and hit me on the legs or across my back, often until I fell to the floor. I never knew what I had done wrong, which made it all the more frightening. But far more often his target was my mother. Every moment when he was in the house she and I both knew that anything she did could be the wrong thing and he would attack. His cruelty and violence were not only physical. He liked to belittle and humiliate my mother, laughing loudly at her and calling her names, or telling her that she was useless. This verbal abuse affected her as much as the physical attacks did. It chipped away at any confidence she might have had, reducing her to a shadow of her former self.

We seldom sat down together at the table to eat or in the lounge to watch television. There was no bedtime routine, no laughter, no games and no discussions. I don't remember anyone reading me a story, or giving me a cuddle. I crept silently and warily around the house, retreating to my room or to corners where I wouldn't be noticed. My father never apologised for his actions and there were no brighter times in between the dark and frightening ones. They just went on and on.

There was no affection of any kind, either between my parents or from them towards us. I never saw them exchange a hug, a kiss, a kind look or warm words. In fact, I think my mother found my father repulsive – I often saw an expression of disgust on her face when she looked at him.

As a small child I felt unloved and unnoticed. I longed to be cuddled, but my mother was far too frightened and traumatised to be able to give me much attention. She was always either crying, distant and withdrawn, or angry. She spent a lot of time weeping in her room, or going silently about her tasks in the house. But sometimes she would become angry and bang pots together in the kitchen sink, as the only way she had of expressing her frustration. I found the noise she made very frightening – she would crash two saucepan lids together and I would run off to hide in the garden or run along the canal bank to escape when she was doing it.

My mother was unable to do more than simply survive, and I just survived alongside her. There was very little meaningful contact or communication between us. But sometimes when she was in bed, recovering from a beating, I would creep in and lie beside her. She didn't seem to mind, at times she didn't even seem to notice. She certainly wasn't able to reach out to me or offer me any reassurance. I would stay for a while and then creep away again, without either of us having said a word.

Neither of my parents did the basic things that most children are able to take for granted; things like cuddling me, getting me dressed and undressed, reading to me, playing with me or even just giving me simple information about what might be happening during the day. I never knew what was going to happen, where my parents were, if they were out, or even when I might be fed.

Although Mum sometimes managed to put me to bed, more often I just took myself off when I wanted to sleep – or to be out of the way. I shared a room with my sister, but we didn't spend time in it together talking or playing. The seven-year age gap was too big for that, and the atmosphere in the house was too oppressive. Most of the time she seemed to have little interest in me, and I had no idea how to reach out to her. So while we both slept there, that was all.

Everything in our house was controlled by my father. He determined who went where and who did what. His favourite among us was Sarah. He encouraged her to go out and to see her friends, so she was very often not around. My brother was reserved, quiet and often distant. My father seemed to have very little interest in him, and this meant that John, too, was out of Dad's way most of the time. John spent a lot of time in his room, with his books. He played the violin and I used to ask him to play to me, because I liked having an excuse to be with him.

I don't know if my father hurt my brother and sister too because I never saw him do so. I always suspected they were scared of him because they were as uncommunicative and silent in the house as I was.

Without doubt, though, Dad took out most of his wrath on me and my mother. Of his three children I was the one, he said, who was most like my mother, and other people have confirmed that I do look very much like her. Perhaps that was why he disliked me so much. Like her, I seemed to irritate and annoy him simply by existing. And like her, I learned to endure the cruelty and the fear and tried not to do anything to draw attention to myself. Silently and anxiously I did my best not to be noticed, because that was the safest way to survive.

I knew, from a very young age, that there was no escape for us and no one who could help. No one would ever believe me if I tried to tell them what was happening, even if I could find the words. My father wasn't some uneducated thug – he was a charming, accomplished, highly educated man with power and influence. As soon as any kind of investigation began he would convince the authorities that I was simply a disturbed child with a vivid imagination. After all, he was an expert on disturbed children.

Running away wasn't an option, either. I knew there was nowhere I could go that he wouldn't find me. He had friends everywhere and he would track me down. My mother knew it, too. She would never have left her children, and with us accompanying her, there was nowhere she could go to find safety. Whatever corner of the country we might try to hide in, he would find us, and would drag us back.

We were trapped in a nightmare with no end. And we knew it.

2

House of horrors

My parents met when my mother, Susan, was eighteen and engaged to a boy she had known for several years. They seemed set on a steady course: they were settled and happy and looking forward to their future together. But then my father blew into her life with the force of a hurricane. Tom Sanders was ten years older than her and he was a football star, goalkeeper for first-division Charlton. Of course, footballers then weren't the demigods they are today. They didn't earn massive salaries or command the kind of celebrity status of today's stars. But even so, playing for a first-division team was a big thing, especially since this was 1966, the year that England won the World Cup. The country was in the grip of football fever and anyone who played the game was a hero.

Perhaps my father's glamorous career was part of the attraction for my mother. He could be magnetic and charismatic and in the early days, before she knew him well, he must have seemed like quite a catch. At any rate,

he swept her off her feet and within days of their first
meeting she had broken off her engagement to her long-
term fiancé. She married Tom on 12 September 1966 –
her nineteenth birthday – just six months after they had
first met.

My maternal grandparents, Helen and James I knew as
Gran and Grandad, didn't have much of a chance to get
to know their new son-in-law, or to discuss their daughter's
plans, because they had moved to the Middle-East a few
years earlier.

My grandfather was a geologist who worked on oil rigs,
and when my mother was sixteen he had accepted a job
in Abu Dhabi, in the United Arab Emirates. He and my
grandmother left my mother and her sister Jane, who was
two years younger than Susan, with their other grandmother. The girls' brother David was a few years younger,
so he went with their parents to Abu Dhabi. They were to
live out there for the next ten years, and although they
made regular visits back to Britain to see their daughters
they were only ever home for a few weeks at a time. There
is little doubt that they had been wary of my father from
the beginning and hadn't been happy about their daughter's
whirlwind courtship. But from such a distance there was
little that they could do.

Although she hadn't wanted to move with them to Abu
Dhabi, I imagine it must have been very difficult for my
mother to see her parents go. Communications then were
less easy and, apart from letters, she could only contact

them via the occasional very expensive – and therefore brief – phone call.

It would be easy to speculate that, with her parents gone, my mother was vulnerable and looking for security when she fell for a man who was older and outwardly successful. But, by all accounts, at that time she was a confident, outgoing young woman, happy with her life and not in the least insecure or vulnerable. In fact she had a strong personality and very clear opinions of her own, and I think this was what attracted my father. Over the years I have learned a lot about perpetrators of domestic violence and, perhaps surprisingly, they are not always attracted to weak, defenceless people, but more often to strong characters. This presents them with a bigger challenge, which they find exciting. Certainly I believe this was true of my father. He didn't pick a wilting flower of a wife – he picked a bright, opinionated girl and set out to break her, physically and mentally.

All that was yet to come, the day my mother walked up the aisle with her tall, handsome footballer. The couple were both from Kent and they bought a house in Folkestone, not far from my father's parents and brother.

My sister Sarah was born a year after they married. My mother stayed at home rather than going out to work. This might well have been her own choice but, judging by my father's reluctance to let her work in later years, it might also have been an early indication of his need to control everything she did.

Not much more than a year after Sarah's birth my mother was pregnant again. By then, it seems, the storm clouds were already gathering over my parents' marriage. During her second pregnancy my mother was, according to a close friend who knew her then, painfully thin and unwell. She later told another friend that my father kept her locked in the house for most of the time, without enough to eat. She was literally a prisoner in her own home and she became seriously malnourished.

John was born in the summer of 1969, a healthy child despite my mother's deprivation. A couple of years later my mother was pregnant once more. This time, a few weeks into the pregnancy, she began to bleed. Whether this was as a result of my father's violence towards her is not known. But what *is* certain is that my father refused to call a doctor or an ambulance and she miscarried.

Through those early years of matrimony friends and family who had known my mother before her marriage saw her change from the happy, confident and healthy young woman she had once been into a pale and withdrawn creature who seemed to have no confidence at all. I have wondered why the people closest to my mother didn't persuade her to leave the marriage at this stage. I can only speculate that either she hid what was happening from them, or they knew, but felt they couldn't intervene. Or perhaps they did try to persuade her to leave, but my mother, believing she must stick it out, refused.

Meanwhile my father was nearing the end of his football

career and he decided to retrain as a physical education
teacher, enrolling for a teacher-training course at Nonington
College near Canterbury.

I was born on 26 February 1974, while my father was
still at the college. As far as I know I was born at home.
I never saw any pictures of myself as a baby, nor any record
of my time of birth or my weight. If these things existed
I never knew of them, and my mother never told me what
kind of birth it was or who was there at the time.

My sister told me that when I was a baby she sometimes
used to come home from school to find me alone, crying
in my cot. No one took any notice or came to me and she
didn't know what to do, so she gave me sweets to try to
comfort me. As early as then things must have been very
wrong in our house. So wrong that, as I learned much later,
while I was still a baby my father drove my mother to a
psychiatric hospital, St Augustine's in Chartham, and left
her there, having told the staff that she was mad. I have
no idea how long she was there, but when I became an in-
patient at St Augustine's myself, after my mother's death,
I discovered what a grim and heartless institution it was
and I often thought about how awful the place must have
been for her.

By the time I was a few months old my father had got
his first teaching job. As well as teaching emotionally
disturbed children, he took them on outings and camping
trips and was closely involved in many of the school's
activities.

Most people think of PE teachers as sporty, friendly and rather laid-back, and this was certainly the image my father projected. But behind this carefully contrived front he was intense, controlling and authoritarian. When I was older I often saw him take pleasure in humiliating and punishing the children in his charge, though never when there were other adults around.

With the new job came a house, so when I was a baby my parents rented out their home in Folkestone and moved to Hythe, close to the school. This was the house I lived in until I was six.

My earliest memories, from around the age of three or four, are of hiding behind curtains and chairs while my father attacked my mother. His violence towards her and manipulation of her was such that it was often impossible for her to manage even the basics of running a home.

Food – or rather the absence of it – probably summed up, better than anything else, the way things were in our home. Sometimes a meal would be served at the table and we'd all sit together. But when we did I was so frightened that I was barely able to eat. I remember once, when I was four or five, being so nervous as Mum served dinner that I dropped my plate of food on the floor. The feeling of dread in the pit of my stomach became almost unbearable as I stared, horrified, at the smashed plate and the food all over the floor. I was sent to bed without anything to eat, but I was so relieved to get away from the table that I didn't mind.

Most of the time there wasn't much food around at all. I would creep into the kitchen to look for something to eat, often scurrying off to eat it somewhere else so that I wouldn't be caught. Sometimes there just weren't any meals, and at other times my mother would send me off to wait until she gave me something to eat.

I don't think anyone set out to deprive me, it was just that the buying and preparing of food simply didn't happen a lot of the time. If my mother made it to the kitchen to cook, my father might well begin attacking her and on those occasions the meal would never reach the table.

It was only at my grandparents' homes that we had nice food. Later, when I was old enough to visit friends, I realised what other families' mealtimes were like. The first time I saw parents and children sit cheerfully to eat together at a table laden with delicious food I was transfixed. And when I found out that they did this every day, and that there was always plenty of food and the children were never hungry, I understood for the first time just how different our family was.

Around the time when I turned four, I began going to a playgroup. It was attached to a Roman Catholic church and to the primary school that I would later attend and which was about ten minutes' walk from home. We weren't Catholics, but my father considered that this was the best primary school in the area. Starting playgroup was a big event as I seldom socialised with other children my age. I remember at first not wanting to go, although I liked it when I got there. On one particular occasion I wouldn't leave my mother at the door and just kept crying because I didn't want her to go. Perhaps not that unusual for a small child, but I hold the memory close because I have so few recollections of her that even a small incident like this is important to me.

I enjoyed playgroup until an incident involving another child – which is still a vivid and powerful memory – changed everything for me. I must have been about four and was playing in the Wendy house. By accident I caught a little girl's hand in the door and she started to cry. The assistant ran over to see what was wrong and comforted the little girl as I stood rooted to the spot, watching. After only a few minutes the girl started playing again. However, I could not play as I was so scared of hurting another person. I walked slowly away from the Wendy house and sat in the corner. I knew I desperately didn't want to hurt anyone like that again, so I decided that I must not play. I also had this huge sense that I must be punished, and since the assistants were not punishing me then it was my job to do the punishing. I remember an assistant coming over to me and telling me that it was not my fault, 'it was only an accident', but this didn't change my determination to punish myself.

I never let myself play again at playgroup, despite the encouragement and concern of the staff. I don't know how long this went on but it was certainly for weeks if not months. Looking back it seems so sad to think of that little girl – me – punishing herself so severely, all because of a small accident for which I wasn't even told off. It seems so extraordinary that a child of four can have such harsh thoughts and then carry through such a self-inflicted punishment for so long. But I did. And it was undoubtedly because my experience of life so far had left me feeling very bad about myself.

Even before this incident, and although playgroup was a nice, friendly place, I wasn't able to relax or to feel truly safe because I was so overwhelmed by what was happening at home. I felt anxious and disturbed because I knew that after a few hours I would be going back home again. In some ways I was like a little robot, going through the motions, internally frozen by what I had been through and the anticipation of what lay ahead. I don't think, however, that I appeared different in any way to the staff. Despite my inner turmoil, I always did what was expected of me and behaved as I knew I should. My anxiety didn't manifest itself in obvious ways – I didn't curl up in the corner or do anything out of the ordinary, I joined in and made sure I was the same as the other children. I never wanted to stand out in any way, though of course after the incident when I accidentally hurt the other little girl I did refuse to play, and this did bring me to the staff's attention. But even then I did my best not to be noticed and to blend in.

At home my father's brutality towards my mother continued and I spent most of my time hiding. My anxiety never lessened because when he wasn't beating her or shouting at her I was constantly on edge, waiting for him to start.

There was no respite when he was out of the house. My mother and I had no shared sense of relief that he was gone. We never relaxed or hugged or chatted. The silent gloom remained, whether my father was in or not, and my fear was so powerful even when he wasn't in the house that I couldn't let go for a moment.

By this time there was another horror to contend with. When I was four my father had begun sexually abusing me – and he was to continue doing so for the next eight years. The first time it happened I was terrified, shocked and bewildered. I didn't understand what he was doing, but I knew it was very wrong.

Even now I find it almost too painful to think about the horrible and frightening things he did, and how much he hurt me. Although I shared a room with my sister he found all kinds of ways of getting me alone – catching me when the other members of the family were out, or taking me on 'outings' in the car. I did everything I could to avoid being alone with him, but he was far too big, strong and clever for me to be able to escape him.

He would warn me that I had to stay quiet. So I would hold my breath and count to ten, because it slowed down my breathing so that I didn't make too much noise. It also helped me to relax my body a little, so that what he did hurt less. I would count to ten over and over again – sometimes it seemed like a thousand times – as he forced himself on me, not letting myself think of anything but the counting. I never managed, as some children do, to disappear into my own world, or pretend that it wasn't happening. It was all too dreadfully real, and I never got used to it. Although I knew deep down that he would never stop, at the same time I clung to the hope, each time, that it would never happen again. So when, inevitably, it did, each time seemed like a fresh shock, as terrible and frightening as the first.

In the same way that I couldn't predict his violent outbursts, I couldn't predict when the sexual abuse would happen, either. The threat was always there, and sometimes he would molest me often, while at other times he might wait for days or even a couple of weeks.

I coped with what he did to me by trying to blank it from my mind after each assault. I felt shocked, sore, dirty and disgusting, but I tried to escape these feelings by consoling myself with my favourite doll, who was called Sally. She had been passed down by my sister Sarah and was far from beautiful. She had short curly brown hair and one of her eyes had been poked out with a pencil, so she looked rather alarming. But what I loved about her was that she was big and – apart from the missing eye – very lifelike. In my fantasies I was her loving mother and she was my age and sometimes a little older. I would take her to school, cuddle her, play with her and make her feel safe and loved. I used to imagine all the little details of our lives – I knew just how everything should be and I would eventually fall asleep still living in this good, clean and happy world that I had invented.

My father didn't often order me not to tell anyone about the abuse – he didn't need to. I knew that I could never say anything to anyone and that no one could help me. My sister was too absent, my mother too traumatised, to listen. At school they would surely pay more attention to an adult than to a child. In any case, sometimes, just to ram the point home, my father would say that if I even told anyone anything he would kill Mum. I knew he meant it and I never breathed a word to anyone until I was sixteen. That was when I managed to tell one other person, and even then I swore them to silence. Before that it was just one more thing I had to endure alone and in silence, one more source of gut-wrenching fear.

As a result of the abuse and my constant state of fear and anxiety, I was wetting my bed. I never told anyone, because I was much too afraid of getting into trouble. I just did the best I could to clean it up. I would get up in the middle of the night and find a towel, wipe myself and then lie on the towel in bed. My mother must have known, because she sometimes changed the sheets the next day, but she never said anything. Like so many other things that happened, it was never mentioned, not because she was embarrassed or was trying to save my feelings, but because there was virtually no communication between family members. I imagine that if my mother happened to notice that my bed was wet, then she would change it, but she

was in too bad a state herself to see that there might be a
more serious underlying problem, or to do anything about
it.

I have always had a very ordered mind and I coped
with all the dreadful things that were happening by sepa-
rating them in my consciousness and focusing on what
was worse. And I was certain that what was happening
to my mother was worse than what was happening to me.
I was terrified that one day my father would go too far
and kill her.

One of the very few sources of warmth, normality and
affection at this stage of my life were my grandparents.
My mother's mother had, by this time, returned from Abu
Dhabi and lived not far away. My grandfather was still
working out there and came home on leave once or twice
a year. Sometimes we would all go over to see them and,
although my father came too, I enjoyed these visits and
liked being at their house. My grandparents had a good
relationship with one another and were loving and warm
with us. I liked to cuddle on Gran's lap, then when she got
up to go and see to the lunch I would immediately transfer
to Grandad's lap. I did my best to stay on one or other of
their laps for the entire visit. They didn't mind, and for
me it was wonderful, I lapped it up like water in a desert.
Not only were there cuddles at Gran and Grandad's, but
the food was always lovely as Gran was an excellent cook.
This was one of the rare times when my father wasn't
dominating the situation. He was polite and fairly distant

with them, but I knew that as long as we were there he wouldn't do anything awful.

It was my mother who did most of the talking to her parents during those visits; she obviously enjoyed being with them and they loved seeing her. But good as the relationship was, they never came over to our house. At the time I never asked why they didn't come to us, or perhaps I understood implicitly that they, like everyone else, were kept outside the grim world of our home. I didn't mind, I was only too happy to go to their house and get away from ours for a short while. But I do wonder what they thought, and whether they questioned why they were never invited.

My other grandmother, Mary whom we called Nan, never came either. She lived not far away from us and my father was very close to her, and to his brother Ted. He was in touch with them on an almost daily basis and when we went out as a family it was most often to see Nan – we went over to her house virtually every week. My paternal grandfather had died before I was born, so I never knew him, but I liked Nan, who was nice and jolly. Like Gran, she always made a lovely meal, and although she wasn't physically affectionate she was kind.

It was very obvious how much Nan cared for her two sons, Tommy and Teddy, as she called them. Ted was a mechanic and she was very proud of both of them and used to make a special meal for them every Saturday lunchtime. Mum didn't often go to these get-togethers, though my sister, brother and I regularly went.

Nan and my mother were never particularly close. They were civil to one another, but there was little warmth between them and no easy chatter. Nan was quite distant with Ted's wife Julie too, so I suspect, like many doting mothers, that she didn't warm to her sons' wives very much.

Ted and Julie and their three children were a nice family, friendly, straightforward and quite gentle. Two of the children were older even than my sister, so they didn't always come to the Saturday lunches. But the youngest, Thomas, was a few years younger than me and I often played with him at Nan's, teaching him little songs like 'Row, row, row the boat'.

Although my father seemed close to his mother and brother, like my mother's family they never came to our house. Even when Nan took me out to the playground or the library, as she sometimes did, she would drop me home without coming in. I wonder whether she questioned it and what she thought – or knew – about my father. Did she suspect what was going on? I just don't know.

It also seems extraordinary – and this struck me when I was very young – that a man who could behave so monstrously came from what appeared to be a loving and very normal family. I felt certain that Uncle Ted was nothing like Dad, and this was borne out when I was a little older and used to go occasionally to stay with Ted and Julie. They were genuinely nice people, as was Nan. So if my father hadn't been mistreated or deprived as a child, how had he turned into the cruel and violent adult that he clearly

was? As a child I had no idea what the answer was. I just
knew that it didn't make sense. It was a psychiatrist who
told me, when I was in my late teens, that my father was
a psychopath with a plausible personality. This does not
mean that he wasn't responsible for what he did, but simply
that the origins of his behaviour were genetic rather than
learned. In other words, he wasn't violent because he had
witnessed violence in childhood, as some people are, but
rather because something was missing in his emotional
make-up.

Psychopaths lack the capacity to empathise or to feel
genuine warmth or love for other people. They also lack
a conscience. And my father was a particularly dangerous
psychopath because he was able to appear – outside our
home – so normal that no one guessed he wasn't what he
seemed to be.

I was four when my father, always heavy-handed and
rough, pushed me over one day in the hall, as we were
about to go to his mother's. I don't know what I had done,
but he gave me a violent shove. I fell on my right arm, and
a searing pain shot through my forearm, so bad that I felt
sick. My father ignored my silent tears as I held my arm
against my body and he took me to his mother's house as
planned, where he dropped me off.

Nan could see that I was in pain, though I don't
remember her asking what had happened. Perhaps my
father had told her that I'd had an accident. She put me
in the bath to try to soothe my suffering but it didn't

help and afterwards I sat in the lounge, unable to move for the agony. Later my father picked me up and took me home. I told my parents how much my arm hurt, but they said it would be better in the morning and I went to bed.

That night I couldn't sleep because of the torment. It was so bad that I did something I would never normally have dared to do and which took all my courage – I went through to my parents' room and woke them. When they saw the state I was in they both took me to hospital. On the way my father told me to tell the doctors that I had fallen over. In the hospital it was confirmed that my arm was broken and it was put in plaster. They were very kind, accepting my explanation that I had fallen, and sent me home with some plaster for my doll, Sally.

That was one of the few occasions on which I complained about pain, so it must have been truly awful. Mostly I had learned not to speak out or make a noise, even when I was really hurting.

One winter, when I was five, snow had fallen and my father decided that we should all go out tobogganing. I was on a toboggan with my mother; I was in front and she was behind, hanging on to me. I was excited, but very scared too, so much so that as we took off down the slope I tried to put my foot down. It got caught under a runner and stayed stuck there all the way down, which was extremely painful, but I simply waited until we reached the bottom. I never thought to scream or try to tell my mother – I was so unused to speaking up or drawing attention to myself that it was as if I didn't know how to. All I knew about was suffering in silence. I had long ago given up any expectation of being heard or comforted, and I had learned that to try to stay safe I must stay silent. When we got to the bottom of the slope my foot hurt so much that I did tell my mother about it, because I knew I couldn't manage another ride. She took me home, but once there she didn't mention it again. I didn't get cuddles and sympathy because those things never happened, when I was hurt or at any other time.

At the age of four and a half I moved up from the playgroup to the school next door, St Augustine's Roman Catholic Primary School. It was a prestigious school and difficult to get into if you weren't Catholic, but my father knew the head, so all three of us children were given places. By the time I got there my sister had moved on to secondary school, but my brother was still there and I remember feeling very proud because he was a milk monitor, which was an honour only bestowed on the most responsible children.

The school was run by nuns, though they had lay teachers too. I liked the head teacher, Sister Anne, who was tall and thin and kind. But my favourite teacher was Miss van Hefton. As well as being very friendly she wore a denim skirt and I thought she was extremely trendy. She also ran the netball team for the top year in the school, and I longed to be picked for it.

Miss van Hefton was often kind to me. Once we were doing a class play about Noah's Ark. Letters had been sent home, asking the parents to provide the costumes, but of course most of the time no one at home read my school letters. When the day arrived for us to bring in our costumes I was the only child in the class without one. Burning with shame, I went to Miss van Hefton and told her that I didn't have one. 'Don't worry, Gayle,' she said, smiling. 'I'll sort one out for you.' And she did, handing me a bright yellow canary mask and costume a couple of hours later. I was so grateful that I wouldn't have to stand out and I liked her from that day on.

I used to be intrigued by what the nuns' hair – hidden under their wimples – looked like, though I never found out. Sister Anne was strict, but I didn't mind that. I was good at keeping to the rules, and I liked her because she used to give me a nice smile when she saw me. I also liked the school secretary, Mrs Dewey, who was lovely to everyone.

At school I quickly learned that the safest place to be in order to attract least attention was in the middle of the class. I wasn't the cleverest or the dimmest, the loudest or the quietest, I just blended in and kept my head down. I was certainly more reserved than most kids, but not enough to cause concern. My main problem was that I found it difficult to concentrate. The desperate anxiety and fear that bubbled just under the surface the whole time made it very hard for me to really hear what teachers were saying, or remember what I was supposed to be doing. But somehow I muddled along and managed to do enough work to avoid being picked out in any way.

The subject I enjoyed most was sport. From the start I was sporty and I was often picked out to demonstrate to the others in gym. I could do handstands and cartwheels and I enjoyed it. The only thing I hated was that being good at PE connected me to my father, because that was his subject.

Sister Anne and the other teachers at my primary school liked my father. His school was close to ours and he often came in to help out with activities – I remember that on one occasion Sister Anne bought him a watch as a thank-you present.

From the beginning I was drawn to a girl called Louise. Her friendly manner gave me the confidence to talk to her a little and we often played together. One day we had a spelling test and we both got stuck on the word 'trousers'. When I went home for lunch that day I asked my mother to write it down on a piece of paper. She did, and I took it back to school, corrected it in my book and showed it to Louise so that she could correct it in hers. I was delighted to have been able to do something for Louise, who was always so kind and friendly to me.

At that time I usually went home for lunch, at my father's insistence, though after the first couple of years I was allowed to have lunch in school. Food was a big issue for me because of the lack of it at home. I usually went to school without breakfast. I'd have something to eat when I came home for lunch, and later there might or might not be some dinner. What food there was would usually be unappetising, and I was often so anxious that I couldn't eat anyway. A lot of the time I didn't even notice that I was hungry because the fear I felt was so huge that there wasn't room for anything else.

I remember coming home from school for lunch one day to find my father at home. He wasn't always there at that time and when I saw him my chest tightened and I wanted to run back to school. Moments later he hit me. He hit me again and I fell. Then he walked away. I had absolutely no idea why he did it. Perhaps I had just come home at the wrong moment. I curled up into a ball, too frightened to cry, and waited until it was time to go back to school.

Even at the age of five I walked most of the journey to and from school on my own. Mum would take me to the main road near our house and see me across, and then I'd walk for the ten minutes it took to reach school. Coming home, I would walk along the road on my own until I saw Mum waiting for me on the other side. I would wait until she told me to cross, and we'd finish the short walk home together.

On one occasion, as I stood waiting by the road, with Mum on the other side, I thought she said cross when in fact she'd said wait. I set off across the road and then turned to see a car coming towards me. Another child might have run, but I froze completely, as I was used to doing at home, and just stood in the middle of the road staring at the car as the driver managed to bring it to a halt just feet from me. Then I turned and carried on across the road to Mum who, having had a scare, was very angry with me.

Because of the way she was suffering herself, Mum could be very angry. She rarely hit me, but she shouted, and I was so constantly nervous that even this was frightening to me.

There was a family next door with a daughter called Katie who was the same age as me. Although none of her family ever came over, Katie would sometimes come and knock on our door and ask if I could play and my mother would say yes. I liked Katie, but it made me nervous when she came into our house. Even if my father was out I would be listening out for the door, only half-concentrating on our game.

One day when Katie was there I was terribly hungry so I asked Mum if we could have something to eat. She said no, but I was so hungry that I sneaked into the kitchen and got two bowls of cereal. Katie and I took them upstairs and went into the bathroom to eat them. My mother found us there and was furious. She slammed the door against the wall, sent Katie straight home and sent me to my room. She was so angry that I never, ever took food without permission again.

It wasn't often that Mum got this angry, so when she

did it made a big impact on me. Most of the time she was quiet, and the anger she undoubtedly felt was vented on the saucepans in the kitchen. But inevitably some of it spilled over onto me and my brother and sister.

School gave my life a tiny taste of normality. But even there my father could appear at any time. Nowhere was safe. My father was everywhere, a presence I knew I could never escape.

Sometimes, with no warning, he would appear in my classroom. He'd say to the teacher, 'Hi, I've come to collect Gayle' and I'd have to get up, collect my things and follow him out. I've no idea why my teachers allowed him to do it: presumably they did because he was a teacher and the interruption was for 'educational' purposes. I think he probably said that as I was good at PE I should have opportunities for extra PE training. No other parent could have got away with it, but because he was friendly with all the staff – and brilliant at persuading people to do what he wanted – he could manage it. After taking me out of class my father would lead me over to his school, next door, to join in the PE lesson that he was giving to the boys.

At other times he would make me get up at five a.m. and take me with him to collect a group of boys from his school. He'd drive the boys and me for forty-five minutes to his old teacher-training college, Nonington, to use the swimming pool. After these morning outings I would arrive to begin the school day exhausted and with wet hair.

I hated and dreaded being taken out of class or forced to go on early-morning swimming trips. I didn't want to do PE or go swimming with a class of boys. But far worse than being thrown in with older boys was having to watch my father's treatment of them. These were vulnerable boys, with a variety of behavioural and learning difficulties, and my father was entrusted with their care and protection. Many of them had emotional difficulties too and they all needed patience and understanding. But my father didn't see things like that. He would force them to take down their shorts and then hit their bare bottoms with a slipper. On one occasion he let them get dressed after a swimming lesson in the open-air pool and then chose one shivering boy and told him to do a handstand at the side of the pool. While the boy was struggling to do it my father put out one finger and pushed him, fully clothed, into the water. Then he laughed loudly at him, encouraging the others to laugh too. When the boy got out of the water he said nothing, and neither did any of the others.

The PE outings were bad enough. I never really understood why he made me join them – perhaps just because he knew I hated them, or because he enjoyed controlling my every move. But far worse were the camping trips. My father would sometimes take me camping at weekends and in the holidays with groups of boys from his school. When this happened he would make us walk all day, miles and miles. Because everyone was scared of my father there was no laughter, no high jinks or mucking about. We walked like little soldiers and then got into our tents at night. I had to share a tent with my father and he would sexually molest me while the boys slept. I'm sure he took me along solely for this purpose, and it was torture.

My father would be the only adult present on the trips – certainly the ones I was on – and this provided him with the perfect opportunity to bully and torment the boys. I don't know why none of the boys reported him. Perhaps he frightened them so much that they didn't dare. Whatever the reason, he got away with it and continued to be perceived as a trusted and caring teacher who generously gave up his spare time to take the boys swimming and camping.

Sometimes Nan would pick me up from school and I was always pleased when she appeared at the gates. She would take me to the library by the canal or to the playground, where I loved going on the swings and the metal horses. These little outings stand out in my memory because they were among the few times when I felt free of fear and was able to enjoy myself. Nan was kind and friendly and I always hoped we could stay out as long as possible before she dropped me home.

Other children looked forward excitedly to Christmas and their birthdays. I never did, because those occasions weren't special or enjoyable in our house. There was never any respite from my father's violence just because it was Christmas or the birthday of one of his children.

I did have a few birthday parties, when most of my class

would be invited. On the face of it these were normal children's parties and I should have been having a lovely time. But I couldn't enjoy them because they were in our house and it had so many awful associations for me. Instead they became like an endurance test. I sat through them, woodenly waiting for the moment when the other children would leave and the horror would begin again.

There was only one Christmas, when I was five or six, when I remember a little bit of magic. On Christmas Eve I was standing in front of the fire in the living room when my dressing gown caught fire. I don't remember being afraid, I simply got it off and my father, who was there, put out the fire. I wasn't hurt, but the dressing gown was completely burnt.

The next morning my Christmas present was a dressing gown. Of course, it must simply have been coincidence that my parents had bought it for me. But I remember thinking that there had to be a Father Christmas for him to have known what I needed and brought it to me. I was certain that no one else could have done it because I had only ruined my dressing gown after the shops had closed.

Small pleasures, like the new dressing gown, were rare and life at home was otherwise relentlessly grim. One day, when I was five or six, I decided that I would run away. My father had been attacking my mother in the lounge and I could hear him snarling insults at her and punching her, followed by her gasps as she fell. Desperate to escape from what was happening I left through the kitchen door, let myself out of the back gate and walked along the canal path that led past the bottom of our garden.

Eventually I came to a bench where an elderly woman was sitting. I remember thinking, 'She's old so she must be tired and that's why she's sitting down.' But I felt she looked nice, too, so I decided to go and sit down next to her. She smiled at me, so, almost to my own surprise, I told her that I was unhappy. She listened, but before she could say anything my brother appeared and said, 'There you are, Gayle – Mum's really angry with you.' I had no choice but to say goodbye to my new friend and plod home behind John.

Back in the house Mum, who must have been in pain from the beating she'd just had, told me sharply never to disappear like that again. Then she went upstairs to lie down. I went to my room, certain now that there really was no escape.

3

No escape

When I was seven my father got a new job. It was a promotion for him – he was made deputy head of a mixed boarding school in Essex for children with emotional and behavioural special needs.

This meant that the whole family had to move. We were given a very beautiful house in the school grounds. I remember being terribly impressed by how grand it was and how big. It was one of a number built in a circle around a driveway, with a grassy area in the centre and the school buildings and fields behind.

Inside, the house had airy, spacious rooms. My parents had a large bedroom at the top of the stairs and John and Sarah each had a slightly smaller one. There wasn't a bedroom for me, so I went between my brother's room and my sister's, sharing sometimes with him and sometimes with her, though most often I preferred John's because I found him easy to be with. He was reading *Lord of the Rings* then, which fascinated me because it was the longest book I'd ever seen. Although he was quiet and distant, I thought a lot of him and liked to be around him. And he didn't mind me being there, although I was never quite sure why, while my presence often seemed to irritate Sarah, who was now fifteen.

Nice as the house was, and although I liked it a lot more than our last home, I never really felt I belonged there because I didn't have a space of my own. It felt temporary and, as it turned out, it was, because we were in Essex for only a year.

All three of us were sent to local schools, my brother and sister to a secondary school and me to Shelley Primary School. I hated my new school. From my first day at Shelley I was miserably unhappy. I made a terrible start when my mother, a firm believer in the value of uniform, sent me in the uniform of my former school, St Augustine's, blazer and all. My heart sank when I arrived at school on the first day and realised that none of the other kids were in uniform of any kind. Despite this I continued to wear it and I didn't argue because I was so used to doing what I was told.

So was my mother, of course, so it may sound strange that she asserted herself so firmly. But despite what she suffered at my father's hands, she could still express strong opinions of her own, and this was one of those occasions on which she did just that. She was undoubtedly a broken woman, in so many ways. And yet, at times, her strength of character would resurface and she would insist that her children should obey her.

I'm sure my mother had no idea of the consequences of sending me to my new school in the uniform, but from the moment I arrived I was at the mercy of the other kids. It was a rough school – most of the other pupils wore jeans and trainers – and of course in my uniform I stood out like a sore thumb, so my classmates called me 'posh'.

The class was well behind the one I'd left, and I'd already covered the subjects, so I considered the work too young for me. Most of the time I just didn't do it, though I managed to stay out of trouble. But what I couldn't avoid was the bullying. There was one boy in particular – he was two or three years older than me and had a twin sister – and he used to beat me up regularly. He would catch me after school and hit me or push me over. In fact, I hardly ever even tried to escape him: I knew he was much bigger and faster and would get me. Nor was I able to defend myself, not only because he was bigger but because I had learned at my father's hands that defending myself just made things worse.

One day he pushed me into a muddy puddle. On another occasion he pushed me into the water fountain and I hit my nose so hard that it poured blood. It was the middle of the day and I went back into school covered in mud, trying to mop the blood from my nose. The pain was so bad that I felt sick – the injury would leave me with a scar on the nose for the rest of my life. But not one teacher said anything or came to help me. I have no idea why this was. At the time I felt that they didn't like me and thought

I deserved what happened to me. Perhaps they thought I was stuck-up and needed taking down a peg or two. Or perhaps it was simply that they couldn't be bothered to intervene or didn't consider it sufficiently serious to address.

I used to try to escape the bully by going to the teacher and saying that I had a headache. I hoped she might keep me in at dinner time. But she would look at me and say coldly, 'I'm not surprised' and then carry on, ignoring me. The message I got, from everyone at the school, was: 'We are not going to help you.'

Conditioned as I was not to complain or draw attention to myself, I bore the bullying in silence. When I arrived back home with a bloody nose, bruises or cuts, no one said a thing and I didn't mention it either. I knew there was no point. Besides, things at home were getting worse. If my father had been violent before, then in Essex his violence escalated to terrifying levels.

One incident in particular, perhaps the worst of that time, has stayed with me. For some reason I awoke in the night and crept down the stairs. As I looked into the lounge from the shadows of the hall I could see my parents. My mother was on the floor on her back and my father was on top of her, choking her, his hands around her neck. She was coughing and struggling, trying to move her arms. Then suddenly he stopped, turned her over onto her front and sat on her back. I could hear her gasping for breath and could see that her face was white. My father grabbed both her shoulders and pulled them back so hard that she went limp. He was forcing them back at such an angle that, although it's probably impossible, I thought I could see her shoulder blades touch at the back.

Terrified that he would see me and not knowing what else to do, I tiptoed back up the stairs and got into bed. I lay there, trembling and unable to sleep, until morning.

The next day I wasn't permitted to see Mum. The door to the lounge was closed and we children weren't allowed in. But I heard her saying to my father, 'I'm paralysed.' I didn't know what it meant, but I knew it must be bad. My father had a nurse he knew come in to see Mum, but he wouldn't let us see her for several days. I worried desperately about what had happened to her and whether she would ever recover.

Eventually Mum appeared, fragile and very stiff, obviously with a lot of pain in her back. It was a long time before she recovered her strength and could move freely.

This same nurse became an ally of my father's. Goodness knows what she made of Mum's injuries – it's hard to believe that she wasn't suspicious. I saw her come and go to and from my mother's room but I never heard her comment. Perhaps my father told her that Mum had fallen or injured herself in some other way. Whatever the case, he certainly won her over with his charm and not long afterwards I heard my mother say to her parents, when we visited them, that my father and the nurse were having 'an affair'. In hindsight, I'm not sure whether she would even have minded. Perhaps the presence of the nurse took a little of the pressure off her: if he was occupied elsewhere then at least, if only for that short time, he wasn't hitting Mum.

But to me it was very puzzling. I remember thinking, 'But the nurse is fat, and Mum's not.' I didn't like the nurse and it didn't make sense to me at all. I used to mimic her – she had huge breasts that seemed to be all over the place – to make Mum laugh.

Despite the affair my father's attacks on Mum continued. On one occasion she was in bed, unable to move after a particularly severe beating, and I went in and sat next to her on the bed. Dad came in and said, 'Don't tell anybody in school' and then added that as a treat I could stay at home that day and look after Mum.

Dad had a favourite pupil in the school, a fifteen-year-old girl whom I'll call Rosie. He took a special interest in her and used to go over to her boarding house to see her. I'm not sure why – I don't know where her parents were – but I could see that Dad seemed to be playing a major role in her life. Perhaps he was given special responsibility for her, which might have been the case if her parents were out of the country. Or perhaps he had volunteered to give her extra educational help. Certainly he never explained to me why Rosie was around such a lot: she often used to come to our house. I liked her and thought that her long blonde hair was pretty. Even though she was eight years older than I was she was very friendly and would always stop and chat to me.

Rosie ran away from school frequently. When she did, Dad would go out looking for her and bring her back. Then one day the police came to our door. I was at the top of the stairs, hiding, and I heard them telling Dad that they had found Rosie running down the High Street, naked. I couldn't imagine why she would be doing this – it sounded so unlikely to me. But of course I never got an explanation because I wasn't supposed to have heard the story in the first place.

A few weeks later Rosie died, in Dad's arms in his office. He told me that she had been sniffing typewriter-correction fluid. I was confused and very upset to think that lovely Rosie was gone. I couldn't understand it: why would someone sniff something so nasty, so much that it would make them die? I missed my friend and I felt certain that something had been very wrong in Rosie's life for her to be running away and sniffing a poisonous substance.

Whatever had happened to Rosie, we moved on from Essex very suddenly and unexpectedly after she died. But although we moved back to Kent my father went on working at the school for some weeks afterwards. A few days after my father said we were leaving I set off for school with instructions to return home at midday, without saying anything to anyone. I arrived back at our house to find the place packed up and we got into the car and set off immediately. I didn't understand why we were going so abruptly but still, I was terribly glad to be leaving that hated school.

My mother, brother and sister were pleased to be leaving, too: we had all been very unhappy in Essex.

It was clear that my parents hadn't been expecting to return to Kent at this point, because we arrived with nowhere to live. Our house in Folkestone was let, so we turned up, with a few suitcases, on my grandmother Nan's doorstep. She agreed that we could stay while my parents sorted out somewhere to live.

It was cramped in Nan's three-bedroom house. I slept on the lounge floor and my brother sometimes slept there with me, while my parents and sister were upstairs. But despite the lack of space I liked staying with Nan and spent as much time with her as I could. I loved her garden, which had apple and pear trees in it. She grew her own gooseberries and tomatoes and I used to go out with her when she was doing the gardening and collecting in her fruit.

Nan was quite adventurous. She used to go on amazing holidays on her own – trips on the *QE2* and Concorde, a safari in Kenya or an exotic Middle East trip – and I liked hearing about them.

I often wished she would give me a cuddle, but she wasn't that sort of person. She was never demonstrative or phys- ically affectionate. But she used to let me do her hair; I would massage in special conditioning cream and comb it through. I think for her this was an acceptable way of allowing contact and, desperate for any kind of touch, I would ask her to let me do it.

While we were under Nan's roof we all joined in the Saturday lunches, and I liked seeing Uncle Ted, who usually brought Julie and my cousin Thomas with him.

One of the best things about being back in Kent was that I returned to my old school, St Augustine's. I was very happy to be back there, in a familiar environment, with my old teachers and my friend Louise. For a few weeks life seemed to be looking a little brighter. My father was still commuting to work at the school in Essex and sometimes stayed there on week nights, so he was around less of the time. And although I was still terribly anxious, while we were with Nan I was less fearful, mainly because my father had to control his violence in front of his mother. At least, it seemed that way – until one awful evening, soon after I had turned eight, when everything changed.

My brother and sister weren't about. Nan and I were sitting at the kitchen table, drinking Guinness. She was filling her glass repeatedly and drinking steadily, and had also given me a little to try. It had this horrible bitter taste, but I felt pleased that she had given it to me, so I kept on sipping it.

While we were sitting there my father began shouting at my mother in the next room. Through the open door I could see him towering over my mother, who was crying. Then he began hitting her, in full view of Nan and me.

Nan seemed stunned, as if she was paralysed by fear. She didn't move, or even acknowledge what we were seeing. As the violence and shouting continued, she started to recall the day my grandfather had died. I knew that he was dead, of course, but not how or when he had died. For some reason she decided to tell me that night, against the backdrop of the violence in the next room.

The night my grandfather died, she said, she had made his supper and was warming his slippers by the fire. This was something she always did as she waited for him to return home after work. I remember her repeating that she liked to warm his slippers and at this point there were tears in her eyes. She seemed to be telling me this story as though she was actually reliving that particular moment. Perhaps she was, and immersing herself in the story helped her to blot out what was happening in front of our eyes.

My grandfather didn't arrive home that night, she told me: he was killed in an accident on his motorbike. She recalled how the police arrived to tell her and all she could say was, 'But he can't have been, he'll be home soon, I'm warming his slippers.' As she spoke she looked so sad, hurt and lonely.

Throughout Nan's recollection of my grandfather's death, my father was still beating my mother. Suddenly he drew his leg back and kicked my mother so hard on the shin that she screamed. I remember the twisting in my stomach and my head bursting with fear. I gritted my teeth, my body stiffened and my mind felt frozen in time. My grandmother and I watched as my mother tried to get up but fell, in agony. My father picked her up, walked past us and took her out into the garden, where he carried on shouting at her and hitting her. My grandmother and I said nothing – we couldn't even look at each other. Nan told me to go bed, where I lay awake until eventually I heard my father dragging my mother back into the house.

The next day my mother's shin was so swollen that I felt sick with disgust and fear. Her leg looked deformed, and she could barely walk.

Nan never spoke of what happened that night, and I can only guess at why she didn't intervene. I imagine she was as scared as I was. Perhaps she thought it was a one-off. Or had she seen my father being violent before? Did she know what he was like because he had threatened her, too? It's hard to think of him growing up without showing signs of the vindictive and violent adult that he was to become. But whatever the answer, as soon as my mother was able to walk we moved out. Whether Nan asked my parents to go, or whether they simply chose to, I don't know. But, having witnessed the horrors of my father's attack on my mother, and perhaps unable to face the truth about her son, Nan must have been relieved when we packed our bags and left.

4

Moments of refuge

With nowhere else to go, we moved into a dilapidated hotel that belonged to a friend of my father's. It had been closed down, presumably because it was in such an appalling state. The five of us were squashed into two filthy freezing-cold rooms, with no electricity, grubby faded wallpaper and damp, musty-smelling bedding on the ancient beds.

Because it had been closed there was no one else in the building – no guests, no staff and not even the owner. It was quite a large hotel and I found it spooky and strange.

From the hotel I had to take a bus to school on my own, as by this time my brother had moved on to secondary school. I'm not sure why my mother didn't go with me: I would have liked her to, but perhaps she didn't think it necessary. I never argued or protested about such things, I just did as I was told.

I managed to get there by asking the conductor to tell me when I was at the nearest stop. But on the way back I realised that I had no idea where to get off. In my panic I got off much too early and had to walk along the main road until I saw buildings that I recognised and managed to find my way back to the hotel.

My parents were obviously anxious to get us out of the hotel, but the tenants in our house in Folkestone were refusing to leave. They were a family with two children who went to the same school as me, but the kids were younger so although I knew them by sight we weren't friends. My father took them to court and the battle raged for some weeks.

Eventually, very oddly, my father was given the right to use one small bedroom in the house. He would go and sleep in this room several nights a week and often took me with him. We'd arrive after dark, make our way up to the bedroom and sleep on the floor in sleeping bags. I couldn't possibly sleep so close to my father and I felt very uncomfortable being in the house with other people whom I didn't know. I lay awake, stiff as a little board, waiting for morning to come. We'd leave the next day without ever seeing the tenants – I imagine they stayed out of my father's way.

While this protracted battle was going on, Nan relented and allowed us to move back into her house. My father must have gone to see her and persuaded her by telling her what awful conditions we were living in at the hotel. Or perhaps he'd convinced her that his violent episode had been a one-off. We were all relieved to be back with her, and on the nights when my father went to the Folkestone house alone and the rest of us were with Nan things were, if not relaxed, then at least a little more peaceful. Mum and Nan were still distant and spoke very little to one another, but there were no rows or upsets.

Sometimes my father decided to take me with him back to Essex, where I discovered that he was spending his free time with the nurse. We'd stay in the nurse's flat with her – sometimes overnight – and it was quite clear that she and my father were intimate with one another. I hated going there and I resented her. She'd attempt to cosy up to me, saying, 'I've put yogurts in the fridge for you', but it only made me hate her more and I'd think, 'I'm not eating your yogurts.'

Eventually the tenants in our Folkestone house – no doubt worn down by my father's regular night-time visits – decided to leave and we moved in the moment they had gone.

This house, where we were to live until my mother's death, was a good-sized semi with four bedrooms and a garden which backed onto woods. The house was on a hill, and on a clear day you could see from the dining-room windows right across the English Channel to France.

I was eight and a half and for the first time I was given my own room. It was very plain and uninspiring, furnished simply and with few concessions to the fact that it was a child's room; just a bed, a chest of drawers and a wardrobe. There were books – my mother was always very keen that

I should read – but I seldom managed to concentrate long enough to read any of them.

I had a few teddies, a white-bunny nightdress case, which lay on the bed and which I loved – and, of course, my doll, Sally. She was the most important figure in my life. I loved her and I spent hours fantasising about her coming to life and being my daughter. I would lie on my bed and imagine the two of us moving out and having a lovely life together in our own home. I had very clear ideas about how she should be looked after and how things should happen in a family.

Sally wasn't my only doll. I had a naughty doll, too. I called her Dob because it was the worst name I could come up with. Unlike Sally, Dob was small. I cut her hair off and didn't let her wear any clothes and I either ignored her or punished her for being bad.

With Sally and Dob I had my own small world. Sally was the depository for all my hopes and dreams. I played with her for hours, creating a perfect world in which she was happy and loved and had lots of attention from her Mum. I taught her things, read to her, played games with her and did school work with her. Sometimes I would put Sally's school work up on the walls of my room. Meanwhile Dob could do no right, and was usually relegated to a corner while Sally and I played. Dob was the one who messed up, got into trouble and who displeased me.

The world I created with Sally – happy, safe and with only a mother and daughter – was the world I wished that

my Mum and I could live in. I knew how things should
be, and how I wished they would be. I think those times
when I played with Sally and imagined the dream world
in my head were my way of escaping from the reality of
my life.

Once we had moved into the house in Folkestone life
continued just as it had before. My father had moved to a
new job in another local school and he continued to torment
and terrorise my mother and me when he was at home.
My mother was more crushed and unhappy than ever and
the two of us would move silently around the house like
two ghosts, seldom communicating, each of us in our own
world of fear and trauma.

Sarah was now fifteen and was hardly ever at home
and John, at thirteen, was also spending a lot of time
out. Neither of them were close to my mother, and it
seemed to me that they weren't supportive or protective
towards her. In fact, they almost seemed to blame her
for what was happening on those few occasions when
they did witness my father's outbursts. But, as I came
to understand when I grew older, and although it may
sound odd, this kind of reaction is all too common
among children caught up in the cycle of domestic
abuse. Desperate for the violence to end, they blame
the victim for provoking the abuser, rather than the
abuser himself.

This is often a tragic twist to what is already a tale of

tragedy, and it was certainly so in our case. As if my mother wasn't suffering enough, she had to face being increasingly alienated from her two older children. Not that I blame them in the least – it wasn't their fault. They were victims too. Our father was always either terrorising us into doing as he wanted, or playing psychological games – in John and Sarah's case, games that were intended to alienate them from our mother.

He didn't try to alienate me from Mum, but he did make sure that we were never able to be close because he was always there between us, and terrorising both of us. Mostly he ignored me, unless he was attacking me. He never asked me about school, homework, friends – or anything else. But he did, sometimes, play a game with me, which he called 'two points'. It was a general-knowledge game in which he'd ask me questions, such as, 'What is the capital of France?' and I would try to answer. I would get two points if I was right and he would get two if I was wrong.

I didn't particularly enjoy this game, but I played it with him because at least it gave me some kind of connection with him that wasn't nasty. During it I somehow felt safer. I would even ask him if we could play and then I'd try to keep the game going for as long as possible, knowing that while he was asking me questions he wasn't doing anything awful to Mum.

John had started to play the piano and our parents had bought one for him. I longed to play the piano too, but although I asked them many times, both my parents refused to allow me to have lessons, or even to touch the piano. Only John was allowed to touch it, although sometimes, when our parents weren't around, he would let me press down one key while he played. He used to play me Christmas tunes and I loved listening to him.

Most parents would want to encourage a child who asked to play an instrument, but not mine. I knew my father's refusal to let me play was vindictive. But it was harder to understand my mother's. She wasn't simply going along with my father: she made it quite clear that she didn't want me to play. She never gave me any kind of explanation or offered to pay for me to have lessons on an alternative instrument, as most parents might. So I was left to work out some kind of explanation for myself, and I decided that perhaps she felt since I was very sporty and John wasn't, he should be the only one to be musical.

Whatever my parents' reasons for refusing, the effect was that I felt punished and disliked, as if I wasn't special or worth anything. But despite this I was never jealous of John. I looked up to him and admired his playing.

The one good thing in my life was being back at St Augustine's, where the teachers were kind and I wasn't bullied. When I returned after my year in Essex, Louise and I were able to pick up our blossoming friendship where we had left off and I was thrilled when one day she invited me home to tea.

From the moment I stepped inside Louise's house I knew

it was just what a family home should be, and that hers was the kind of family I would love to have had. Her home was warm and inviting and her relatives were kind and friendly. They all chatted to each other and swapped news and everyone seemed relaxed and at ease.

When we arrived after school, her Mum took us into the kitchen, where she'd made a plate of sandwiches and put out crisps and glasses of squash for us. That was just for a snack, she told us. Tea would be coming later.

I asked Louise if her Mum had put out the food because I was coming. Louise said no, and told me that her Mum did that every day. I was embarrassed that I had thought anybody might do something special for me, and at the same time amazed at the information that this was an everyday event. It was hard for me to believe that inviting plates of food were put out just so that everyone could help themselves, and at first I hesitated to take a sandwich.

Louise's Mum, Dad and older sister Rachel all made me feel welcome. Louise also had a dog, a collie called Fia. She was very beautiful but she barked whenever I was at the door, which alarmed me as I wasn't used to being around pets.

After that first time Louise often asked me to tea. I loved being at her house. I was always fed well and treated with kindness. Sometimes Louise's Mum would give us some money to go to the bakery down the road. We'd stand at the counter, looking at all the delicious goodies on display, but despite all the many mouth-watering options, in the end Louise always had a sausage roll and I always had a doughnut.

I never wanted to go home, but eventually I had to leave the safety and warmth of Louise's house for the bleak misery of mine. I walked, or sometimes Louise's Dad would drive me, the mile home.

I was reluctant to invite Louise to my house, but I realised that she and her family might think it odd if I didn't. So I asked her and during the next three or four years she came over a number of times, though far less often than I went to her house. At my house there were no inviting plates of sandwiches or glasses of squash and no delicious tea to follow. Louise always went home when it was time for tea.

I took her to my room, where we played quietly. Although I enjoyed her being there, I was in a state of high alert, hoping desperately that Dad wouldn't do anything awful while Louise was there. It took me a while to realise that he wouldn't, because Louise might have told her parents and then the truth would have been out. My father wouldn't have wanted to risk that. Once Louise had gone he might well launch himself at my mother, slamming her into the wall and twisting her arms. But as long as a guest was in the house he controlled himself. And in fact he liked Louise, calling her 'the jam-jar kid' – a play on her surname, James. With her he was usually friendly and cheerful and she would have had no reason to suspect that he was anything other than a nice Dad.

My friendship with Louise remained strong and her home became a refuge for me. From the age of eight I used to walk over there by myself. Mostly I hadn't been invited – I would just turn up. I was always made welcome and often stayed over on Saturday nights. Louise and I would curl up in front of our favourite TV programme, *TJ Hooker*, with a snack and a drink, brought to us by her Mum.

Louise's family liked one another, enjoyed doing things together and had fun. I have very few memories of my own birthdays, which were torturous affairs, but I can remember every one of Louise's birthdays. While I merely went through the motions of having a party, which was a tense, miserable and regimented event with my father looming over it, Louise's parties were original and exciting.

On her eleventh birthday six of us girls went to a health club and had our first sauna, all giggling in our swimming costumes and daring each other to take our tops off. For her twelfth birthday her father took me, Louise, and another friend to a Chinese restaurant and left us there to order for ourselves. We ordered a mountain of food and had a wonderful time trying – and failing – to eat it all. I wondered if Louise's Dad would be angry when he came back and saw the bill, but he just laughed and said, 'That's OK, baby.' I could hardly believe that a parent, even Louise's Dad, who I knew was a kind man, could be so generous.

Much as I'd have liked to spend my whole time at Louise's house, I couldn't. And apart from my time with her there was precious little respite from home. I did still see my grandparents, and I always welcomed our visits to them. And I saw my Uncle Ted and his family.

Ted was always cheerful and good fun. One day, when I was nine, Mum and I were walking home from town after I'd had a haircut when we bumped into Ted. He said he was going for a swim in the sea and asked me if I'd like to go too. It wasn't summer and the weather was quite chilly, but I liked being with Ted and I said yes. I grabbed my swimming things and we set off for the beach. On the way Ted took my hand and sang 'I wanna hold your hand'. And at the beach we had a lovely time jumping in and out of the freezing waves. That afternoon became a precious memory of one of the very rare carefree moments in my young life.

We also used to go and see my mother's brother and sister, and I always enjoyed these visits. Jane, her husband Mike and their three boys lived about eight miles away, in the Dover area. We'd sometimes go over and see them for the afternoon. James, the oldest of their boys, was the same age as me and we got on very well – we'd disappear upstairs to play while the adults talked downstairs.

We always went as a family, I think partly because Mum didn't drive and she needed my father to take us. She loved her sister and I always had the impression that she'd have liked to see her more often. I would have liked to as well – I sometimes asked if we could go and see Jane's family.

The only time I ever saw my parents together in company

was when we visited their respective families. With my father's family he was the chatty one, while my mother was quiet. And with her family it was the other way around. Mum would be more talkative and outgoing than she ever was at home, while my father would say very little.

I remember once, when I was about seven, my parents and I walked over to Jane's house. I have no idea why; perhaps it was a whim of my father's. It was in the evening and when we arrived James was in his nightclothes. Jane asked me if I'd like to borrow some of his pyjamas. I thought that was very funny, as they were boys' ones, but I said yes and he and I sat in his bed reading a book. Later on his Mum came and asked me if I'd like to stay the night. I really wanted to, but I didn't dare say so as I was sure that my father wouldn't allow it, so I just said, 'No, thank you.' I got dressed again and we got the bus home.

We also used to go and see my mother's brother David and his wife Holly. They lived in Tunbridge Wells and had a son and daughter, both much younger than me. We didn't see them as often as we saw Jane's family – I think my mother was closer to her sister – but I always liked them and enjoyed our visits.

I liked seeing my mother brighten up when she visited her family, because it was such a contrast to the way she was at home. She and my father barely spoke when he wasn't attacking her, and she continued to spend much of her time in bed, either weeping or deep in depression.

* * *

Around this time, when I was nine, we suffered a series of burglaries which added hugely to my state of terror. The burglars were so audacious that they seemed to think it was funny to taunt us. On one occasion we came downstairs in the morning to find that they had been drinking glasses of milk and eating biscuits at our kitchen table – the empty glasses and biscuit crumbs were evidence that they'd taken their time and enjoyed themselves.

Another time I woke to hear someone outside my room. I lay so still that I was barely breathing, my heart hammering inside my chest, as someone came in. I squeezed my eyes shut, praying they would leave me alone. Thankfully they must have decided that a child's room was of no interest because they left a few moments later.

On yet another occasion my father woke while they were in the house and gave chase, catching one man in the road outside and hanging on to him until the police arrived.

In addition to the terror induced by these burglaries I was watching a lot of frightening television. Because the two adults in the house generally ignored me, I was left to my own devices and went to bed very late. My father often went out and my mother was frequently in bed. My brother and sister would be out too, or in their own rooms, so I'd stay up to watch *Hammer House of Horror* alone, even though it scared me dreadfully.

The combination of the burglaries and the films, in addition to the daily real-life horrors I witnessed at home, left me so afraid that I became convinced that I was going to be murdered, either by my father or by one of the burglars. Sometimes, especially at weekends or in the holidays, both my parents would be out. They never went out together and neither of them ever told me where they were going, or when they would be home. My brother and sister were often out too, so I would find myself alone in the house with no idea where they all were or when anyone would come home.

At times like this I would barricade myself in the living room. I would move all the living-room furniture, including the sofa, across the doors and I would spend the whole day in the room, preferring not to eat or visit the loo, rather than venture out. I used to sit on the sill of the room's bay window, watching for one of my parents to return, muttering, like a mantra, 'Please don't hurt me', over and over again.

As soon as I saw my father arriving back in the car, or my mother walking up the hill, I would move the furniture back into place, so that I wouldn't get into trouble.

Tormented and terrified as I was, I knew that my mother was suffering far more. My father continued to abuse and attack her regularly, and I could see in her eyes and in her body language the depth of her suffering. She was a broken woman, worn out, desperate, utterly frustrated and trapped. When she was out of bed she was usually angry. I was desperate for affection from her, but she simply wasn't able to give me anything. She was drained, empty, unable to do anything but function at a very basic level and go through the motions of doing her hair, putting on make-up and dressing neatly in skirts and jumpers.

She seemed to be angry more often now and I found her outbursts frightening. She had begun grinding her teeth a lot and she would still bang saucepans together and even smash plates at all sorts of odd times, including the middle of the night. I'd wake to find all the lights on and Mum in the kitchen, crashing pans together or throwing crockery on the floor, her face tense with fury. Sometimes she seemed almost to be in a trance: she'd stand at the sink, banging a saucepan up and down, holding it with both hands, bashing it over and over again, barely aware of what she was doing. I'm certain that she had no idea of the effects of her behaviour on me – she probably wasn't even aware of my presence. Strangely, my father never said anything to her about it; he just appeared to ignore it.

There was, though, one point of connection with my mother that I had found and which gave me an opportunity to share some moments of closeness with her. She loved to take baths, and would frequently lie in the bath for ages. Sometimes I would tap on the door and ask whether I could get in with her. She often said yes, and I would take off my clothes and climb in at the other end of the bath and sit there with her, both of us silent. I went on doing this until I was ten or eleven. Those shared bath times were the nearest we ever came to intimacy and I treasured them.

My father's violence towards her became increasingly spooky. While he would regularly erupt and lash out at her, he was also cold, calculating and intimidating. He would humiliate her by laughing at her, a loud, roaring, exaggerated laugh. If she became angry he'd always jeer at her. At other times he'd stare at her, his eyes following her every move, saying over and over again in a slow, menacing voice: 'You're mad, you're mental, bad, evil, no good.'

He also had a very sinister admiration for Adolf Hitler, whom he would often quote or refer to with undisguised approval. At first I didn't know who Hitler was, but after I learned I was shocked that my father clearly thought he was someone to admire.

I have no doubt that my mother found my father repugnant in every way. Despite his well-turned-out appearance he didn't wash regularly and he often smelled strongly of body odour. Although she said nothing, I could see that my mother was disgusted by everything about him and couldn't bear to be near him.

Both she and I were my father's prisoners, trapped and vulnerable, not just at home but wherever we went. Such was his power that I felt our situation was hopeless. The older I grew the more certain I became that he would eventually kill one or both of us.

For my mother the frustration and despair must have been overwhelming. Year after year she had suffered at his hands, and in that time she must have gone over in her mind – many, many times – what her options were. Once she'd had children she must have felt that there was no escape. She had no income, no place to go and no way of surviving. She couldn't drive, so even the physical act of leaving would have been difficult, with her children and, at most, a few suitcases. Refuges for battered women had been in existence for almost a decade by this time, but whether she had heard of them, or had ever considered trying to get to one, I don't know.

However, despite suffering eighteen years of beatings, humiliation and torture, my mother's spirit was not entirely crushed. Though she appeared passive in the face of her torment, she was still searching for a way out. And when I was ten, she began to fight back.

5

My mother fights back

What prompted my mother to act after so long, I don't know. But I think my father's violence had become so bad that she grew convinced he would kill her if she didn't find a way to leave. It is also possible that someone encouraged her to act. She did have a friend she used to visit, and perhaps she confided the truth to this friend, who urged her to get away.

Whatever it was that motivated her, my mother made up her mind to get both herself and me away. And she decided to do it not by running away and risking him tracking her down but by using the proper legal channels. Astonishingly, and very bravely, given how controlling and violent he was, she planned to file for divorce and to win custody of me so that she could take me with her.

Her first step was to gain herself some kind of independence, which meant getting a job. My father had always been fiercely opposed to her going out to work, so this was a brave move. Perhaps, as well as gaining a small income for herself, she saw it as a way of testing his reaction before she moved on to confront him with her demand for a divorce.

The first job she found was as a receptionist on a caravan site for holidaymakers, not far from where we lived. When she was offered the job she was thrilled. She started work there but soon afterwards she was told, with no explanation, that she was no longer needed. 'It's him, it's him,' she sobbed, after receiving the news. I had no doubt that she was right. My father seemed to know everyone in the area and could well have contacted her employer.

She didn't give up. Instead, she decided to go back to studying and improve her educational qualifications, something my father couldn't stop her doing unless he locked her permanently in the house. Her hope was to become an English teacher and she attended a local college part-time for the next couple of years.

This must have been an enormous step for her to have taken. Crushed and isolated as she had been for so long, I think it extraordinary, looking back, that she found the strength and courage not only to go against my father but to face a new situation, with new people and the challenge of study. But this was the paradox of my mother: on the one hand a battered wife, broken and subdued, and on the other still a spirited, strong woman who would not give in. Hard as my father tried to control her every move – and I'm certain that he did – he never fully succeeded.

I am sure my mother paid the price for her rebellion,

through my father's cruelty and violence. But she was not going to be deterred: she had found the courage to pursue a way out of the hell we lived in, and she was going to carry on.

And I think she enjoyed going to college. Though nothing improved at home – it was as grim and frightening as ever – there was sometimes a spring in her step which hadn't been there before. I was glad of those moments when she appeared happier, even though I didn't believe that what she was doing would free us. My conviction that we were stuck in a living hell was unshakeable.

After a few months she decided to apply for another job, this time as a doctor's receptionist, and on this occasion my father didn't manage to stop her. No doubt she'd looked for a future employer whom he wouldn't know. She enjoyed the work and this part-time job led to another, in the local hospital. I have always found doctor's receptionists to be very nice people, kind and helpful, and I wondered if my mother could summon up a new spirit when she did the job.

Around this time, when I was just ten, something happened which, with hindsight, might well have been a significant factor in Mum's decision to file for divorce. My father was still regularly sexually abusing me. I had never told anyone – it didn't even occur to me to do so, as I was far too frightened of the consequences. But one day, after another brutal assault, I went to the loo and saw blood in my knickers. This hadn't happened before and it shocked and frightened me.

I didn't know what to do, but I realised that I had to find a way of letting someone know. Later that day, Mum and I went to Nan's house. I'm not sure why we were there, because Mum and Nan still had a cool relationship and Mum didn't often visit on her own. Perhaps we were waiting for my father to arrive. Whatever took us there, Mum and Nan were sitting together in the lounge drinking tea and eating Rich Tea biscuits. Without saying a word, I walked in, pulled down my trousers and knickers and showed them the blood. It was so unlike me to do something like that; usually I hated drawing attention to myself. But I was really scared by the blood and needed to tell them.

I could see clearly by the looks on their faces that my mother and Nan were shocked. Mum told me to get dressed again and promised to take me to the doctor, but otherwise she said nothing to me about it.

The visit to the doctor came a couple of days later. He asked me to undress and lie down, and I was so anxious and tense that Mum said to me, 'Gayle, it's all right, you need to relax.' It was the only time I ever remember her saying something like that to me. The doctor examined me and asked, 'Has anybody done anything to you?' Desperate though I was to say yes, I didn't dare. In a small voice I said no, and the doctor, with not a single further question, nodded and said, 'OK, then.'

I've no idea what the doctor discussed with my mother as I waited outside, but nothing more was said by either of them to me. I realised that no one was going to do anything about it and that unless I told them what my father was doing the whole matter would be dismissed.

Although my mother never said another word to me about it, and took no steps to protect me, I later learned that she did indeed suspect my father. Some time later, during their custody battle over me, she expressed these fears to the court-appointed Welfare Officer. I wasn't to discover this until many years later when I was able to look through the social-services file on my case.

Knowing that Mum did suspect the truth – and with a very tiny, physically immature ten-year-old girl who hadn't started menstruating, it would have been hard not to – I wonder what part it might have played in her decision to leave my father and take me with her. Certainly it was not long afterwards that she told me she had gone to a solicitor and filed for divorce and that she was determined to win custody of me.

I knew how courageous a stand this was. For years Mum had been doing everything she could not to exacerbate my father's violent behaviour. She had learned to modify her own behaviour so that she didn't argue with him, express an opinion or even discuss anything in his hearing. She was quiet, avoiding anything that might have been seen by him as provocation. Yet now she was flying in the face of all this caution with a move so daring that it is hard to imagine how she felt able to do it.

She was well aware of what she was up against, and knew that my father might stop at nothing to prevent her walking away and taking me with her. But she was prepared to risk everything for the chance of freedom.

I was both shocked and worried by Mum's decision. While she must have felt a degree of optimism, I didn't feel at all excited or hopeful. In fact I felt certain that she would not succeed. I simply couldn't imagine our situation changing. My father was so controlling, manipulative and powerful that I was sure he would never let us get away. I felt hopeless and resigned, as well as fearful that he would hurt her – or both of us – in some terrible way.

Initially my father seemed to take the news of my mother's filing for divorce surprisingly well. I don't think he looked on it seriously, or believed she'd go through with it. He reacted by getting his own solicitor and determining to beat my mother at her own game, which meant succeeding in the one thing that would truly hurt her – winning custody of me.

He must have been told of the incident when I had shown Mum and Nan the blood in my knickers. He must also have been given permission to obtain his own medical report on me because one day he ordered me into the car and took me to a hospital. We went to see a male doctor who ordered me, in a very matter-of-fact voice, to take off my knickers and stand on a chair. I felt horrified and humiliated, but I had no choice. My father stood glaring at me as I removed my underwear slowly and climbed onto the chair. I had no idea why I was standing there while the doctor came over and looked at me before asking, 'Is there anything you want to tell me?'

Unable to speak, I shook my head and he told me I could get dressed again. Like the doctor my mother had taken me to see, this one appeared uninterested and showed absolutely no sensitivity or concern for me. And once again I was questioned in front of a parent – this time the offending parent – so how on earth could they imagine that I could have said anything?

I hated the thought of whether or not I had been abused being discussed in court. I felt disgusted and humiliated just thinking about it. And of course no one ever told me what the doctors' conclusions were. I imagine that, as I made no actual allegation, and all they had to go on was my mother's suspicion, which could have been interpreted as vindictive, the matter was dropped. It would have taken a direct allegation by me, backed up by a full and thorough medical examination – which was never carried out – for official action to have been taken against my father.

As time went by my father realised that my mother was serious about divorcing him and he became more and more agitated and antagonised. Mum was doing things for herself, and recovering some of her lost confidence. She saved up and bought herself some new clothes – something I had never seen her do before – and she went out more often.

My father reacted to all this with growing fury, and as he watched her gaining more control over her life and felt his own grip on her slipping, his violence and emotional abuse escalated. Yet his frequent and terrifying attacks didn't stop her. In fact, she seemed increasingly determined to go through with it.

Watching all this, I felt a deepening sense of impending doom. I was quite certain that there could not be a positive outcome, and I couldn't believe that my mother really thought we might get away. I had a more and more powerful sense of waiting for something terrible to happen, and feeling utterly helpless and unable to stop it.

I'm not sure how my brother and sister felt about the imminent divorce. It wasn't something that either of them talked to me about; ours was not a family in which things were discussed or even acknowledged. John and Sarah were, by this time, fifteen and seventeen respectively and the custody issue did not concern them as by the time a divorce could be granted they would be at least sixteen and eighteen and free to decide their own futures.

Sarah was, as ever, out most of the time. She'd had a boyfriend since she was thirteen and she preferred to be at his house. John spent lots of time out too, but I saw more of him than I did of Sarah. There were times when our parents were both out – they never told us where, as I've already said, but presumably our father would go to school meetings and Mum would go to see her friend – and John and I were the only ones at home. I was still getting very scared at night, and I would go along to John's room and knock on the door, begging him to let me come in and wait with him until Mum came home. He usually said yes, and he'd let me sit in the corner of the room while he worked or went to bed. At other times he'd tell me to go to bed, but would leave his door open to reassure me.

Both Sarah and John accompanied our father to court. I never talked to them about it; like so many other things, it was just never discussed. But I knew the power our father had, and that he could have pressurised them to do it. He forced all of us to do what he wanted, and Sarah and John were his victims as much as Mum and I were.

When I think of the way my father manipulated us I am reminded of cases in which a child has been kidnapped by a stranger and then been brainwashed into staying with them, despite being able to leave. I read the story of a young boy in the United States, kidnapped at the age of eleven, who spent four years with his kidnapper only a few miles from his childhood home. This boy had considerable freedom of movement and could have escaped, so after he was rescued many people drew the conclusion that he had chosen to stay and had preferred his kidnapper to his parents.

I knew how untrue this was, and realised that what the story actually showed was the extraordinary level of control that the kidnapper had exerted over the boy. Such powerful control that he was able to allow the boy to come and go, knowing that he would never run away. This is the ultimate control of the perpetrator: not locking someone away, but having such a hold over them that he can allow them to appear free.

I believe that this was the kind of control that my father wielded over all of us. And I think this was how he was able to make all three of his children do exactly what he wanted. He loved playing with people as though they were pawns in a game of chess. It excited him.

In her new job, Mum worked at the hospital several days a week, including Sundays. On that day I used to walk down the hill to meet her bus after she had finished. On the way I'd sometimes drop in to see Nan. Mum had stopped visiting her once the divorce was in progress, but I was fond of her and didn't want to lose touch. After that I'd meet Mum and we would go over to my other grandparents. Dad no longer came, and my brother and sister seldom came either, now that they were older.

We'd spend the late afternoon and early evening with Gran and Grandad and I always liked this time. When my mother was with her parents and my father wasn't around she was a different person. That was the only time I heard her laugh, or talk freely. She would chatter away to them while I played or watched television and I would listen, fascinated. This was a person I didn't know at home. I felt sad that I so seldom saw her like that. I loved hearing her laugh; she had an unusual high-pitched laugh which was distinctive.

Mum would have a drink and relax. She really enjoyed

a glass of sherry or a Martini and lemonade, accompanied by a handful of salted peanuts or, her other favourite treat, some Cadbury's Dairy Milk chocolate. My father never drank and declared alcohol to be evil, though, perhaps surprisingly, he didn't object to Mum having the occasional drink at home.

Mum was close to her parents and confided in them. I doubt that she had ever told them about the degree of violence to which she was subject from my father, knowing it would have distressed them. But she must have told them that she was divorcing him and a little about why, and it certainly seemed as though they approved of her decision.

Mum seemed to look on her visits to her mother and father as a chance to escape the horrors of her own home and enter a saner, safer and more welcoming world. As the evening wore on we would settle down to watch *Howard's Way*, a TV family saga which was compulsive Sunday-night viewing for most of the country and which we loved. Towards the end of the programme Mum would grow quieter and I would feel my insides tensing as our inevitable departure grew nearer. When the programme ended we put on our coats and said our goodbyes. As we sat on the bus in silence, the chatter, laughter and warm atmosphere we had left behind evaporated and cold dread filled us both.

Once we were back inside our front door we parted again. I would creep off to my bedroom to play with Sally, or to the living room to watch television, while my mother would go about her housework, both of us knowing that it was just a matter of time before the next onslaught began. Sometimes my father would launch into my mother, furious that she had dared to be out of the house all day – he hated her doing anything for herself, and working and visiting her parents were both in this category. He would attack her as I cowered nearby or upstairs, desperate to help her and knowing that I couldn't. Even if I had dared to try and phone for help I couldn't have, as by this time he had put a padlock on the phone and none of us – including my mother – could use it.

From the very beginning the divorce was a battle between them, one that hinged mainly on custody of me. I felt I was being used as a pawn. And from the start my father, arrogant and self-assured, was certain that he would win. After all, he was the one with good standing in the community. He was the one who knew all about children, and was seen as a devoted teacher and father. And he was the one who had influential friends, while my mother had nothing and no one.

In addition, as I came to see, he was portraying my mother to his friends as a mentally unbalanced woman who made his life hell, while he, of course, was the patient, loving husband, doing his best to cope.

The events which really brought this home to me happened one afternoon when I was just eleven. I had come in from school and was upstairs in my room when I heard my father's raised voice, and then my mother's. I wanted to hide, but then my father called me and I didn't dare disobey.

My parents were on the front lawn. As I stood in the doorway I could see that my mother was brandishing a carving knife at my father, who was jumping from side to side and laughing loudly. Her face was red and her eyes were puffy from crying, while my father clearly thought the whole thing was a big joke. I knew he had probably been hitting her and – most unusually – she'd retaliated by picking up the knife to fend him off.

After a few seconds my mother spotted me and shouted, 'Gayle, get in the house.' But before I could move my father shouted, 'Gayle, get in the car.' I stood, paralysed, as they both shouted at me over and over again, until my father came over to where I was standing, picked me up and put me in the car. After that he jumped in beside me and drove off. I could still hear my mother calling me, but there was nothing I could do. I felt so terribly guilty, as though I was taking his side, when in fact I wasn't at all. I was just too scared to object.

My father drove us to the house of one of his friends, the local vicar. I heard him telling the vicar about his awful wife, how she was deranged and had threatened him with a knife. Then the vicar came in to where I was, led me into another room and sat me down. In his most soothing voice he said to me, 'Tell me what's happened. I understand your mother isn't well. Is it true that she was in the garden with a knife?'

I didn't know what to say. My father was in the next room and I felt his presence, controlling the whole situation. I wanted to explain that although my mother had been in the garden with a knife, that wasn't the whole story, and she wasn't mad. But in the end I was so frightened of my father that all I could manage to say in answer to the vicar's question was yes.

I felt I had betrayed her, and the feeling grew worse when my father came in and said, 'You see, my daughter has had to witness her own mother behave in this appalling way', as the vicar nodded sympathetically. This was what my father did to win people over. Both he and my mother had begun attending this vicar's church during the previous year or so. I have no idea why they both decided to go at around the same time. They didn't go together, they sat on opposite sides of the church and didn't even acknowledge one another. My mother took me with her, but I hated going. I felt embarrassed that my parents weren't sitting together and I found the service boring.

I knew that Mum had been to the vicar for help, hoping that he might support her in escaping her terrible situation. But her pleas must have fallen on deaf ears; it was very clear who the vicar believed and whose side he was on.

Later we returned home, my father with a smug little smile of satisfaction on his face at another victory scored, me with my head bent, feeling desperate guilt and misery. My father didn't care in the least – he used whatever and whoever he had to in order to get what he wanted. At home my mother had gone, weeping, to bed. I climbed the stairs and crawled into my own bed, feeling utterly wretched.

This was to be one of many occasions during the ensuing divorce and custody battle when my father would use me to help him build a case against my mother. He was clever and knew just how to manipulate people, and he also knew that I was far too frightened ever to disobey him, no matter how terrible I felt at letting my mother down.

By the time the divorce was on its way through the courts I was beginning my final year in St Augustine's. My teacher, Mrs Wiggins, was cheerful and motherly and I still had a strong friendship with Louise, so school was in many ways my refuge from home, despite my father's frequent appearances there. And to my delight I was now the captain of the netball team. Miss van Hefton, my second-year teacher, who also coached the team, had invited me to join a year early, when I was ten, and I loved it. I never missed a practice or a match – netball gave me something to focus on other than fear and anxiety and for those brief periods while I was playing I was able to lose myself in the exhilaration of hard physical activity.

At school we had to have eye tests every year. My eyes had always been fine, but in the test that year it seemed that my sight had deteriorated so much that I needed glasses. As this was rather sudden, a second test was carried out. This time my sight was perfect. Puzzled, the school nurse tested me again several times. Each time the result

was different – sometimes I needed glasses, at other times
I didn't.

The school suggested that Mum should take me to an
optician in Hythe, which she did. After testing me and
getting the same contradictory results he said, 'This doesn't
really make sense. Is there something that is making you
not see sometimes?' He went on to ask whether there were
any problems at home that were making me feel upset, and
to suggest that if so there might be times when I felt unable
to see.

Unfortunately he talked to me in front of Mum, and
although I liked him and could see how perceptive he was,
I didn't feel able to say anything. So I told him that everything was fine. I think he might have pursued it, but the
conversation was cut short because I had to get back to
school for a netball match.

Eventually I was referred to Moorfields Eye Hospital to
see if they could work out what was going on. Mum took
me along and the doctors there were both confused and
intrigued by my wildly differing test results. But they
couldn't come up with any answers. They decided not to
give me glasses and to leave me and re-test me a year later.

That sensitive optician had, I'm certain, rightly suspected
that something at home was badly wrong. To me it made
perfect sense that I might unconsciously choose 'not to see'
sometimes; I spent most of my life trying to avoid seeing
what was going on at home. But I suppose neither the optician nor the doctor who had questioned me about the blood

in my knickers felt they could do much when I insisted that everything at home was fine. And with my mother beside me and my father's threatening presence looming over both of us, what else could I do?

6

Losing the battle

In the months leading up to my parents' divorce the two of them became locked in a protracted and vicious battle over custody of me which left me feeling even more frightened and anxious than before.

Far from feeling loved or wanted by either of them, I felt that I was a tool in a power struggle. But while I am certain that my father didn't love me, I think my mother must have, because otherwise she could have left me with my father and escaped. She stayed for me, and that tells me she cared. I think she was simply so overwhelmed and traumatised that she was unable to pay me any attention, or show me affection. I do believe that on her side the battles were fought in what she genuinely felt was my best interest, while I am certain that my father never truly wanted me – he simply wanted control over both of us. But whatever the truth of it, being tugged back and forth by the two of them in a grim and merciless war was agonising.

One of the reasons why I felt so unloved was that although I was the subject of the dispute, neither of them ever asked me how I felt, or what I would like to happen. Neither of them put an arm around me, acknowledged how tough things were or offered me any comfort. Despite each of my parents' efforts to gain ultimate control of me and my life, my feelings, thoughts and needs appeared to be utterly insignificant.

In the build-up to the divorce the court appointed a Welfare Officer, a very pleasant social worker called Dawn to advise on what should happen to me. Both my parents had to make submissions to her, and this was a cue for my father to play every dirty trick he knew. He forced me to write letters to the Welfare Officer about how awful my mother was. This was torture for me, but I was just too frightened to disobey him. One of the letters I wrote was on some yellow notepaper I had been given, which had little bananas decorating the border. I really liked that paper, but as I sat over it, toying with my pen, my father beside me, I began to hate it. Eventually, my hand trembling, I wrote: 'My Mum's not very nice.' Desperate to water it down I added 'a little bit'. My father looked at it and ordered me to rewrite it, changing 'a little bit' to 'a lot'. Then he made me add: 'I think it's bad that she swears.' Satisfied, he took it to deliver to the Welfare Officer.

Though she never mentioned them, I knew my mother would hear of this letter and others he forced me to write, and I felt upset and guilty. The letters were completely untrue: I loved my mother and wanted to be with her. But I was far too scared of my father to refuse his bullying demands.

The Court Welfare Officer was a nice woman, as I've said, and she asked me who I wanted to live with. I couldn't say I wanted to be with my mother – I knew my father would hear of it and would punish both Mum and me – so I said I wanted to be with both my parents. The records kept by social services record their impression that I felt torn and wanted my parents to stay together. I didn't, but I believed that was the only hope I had of keeping in touch with my mother. I knew, even then, that my father would never let my mother take me. So I clung to the straw of hope that if they stayed together I could at least be with her, even if the price was that we both had to be with him too.

Despite what I told them, and the letters that my father forced me to write, the recommendation of the Court Welfare Officer and of the social worker assigned to the case was that custody should be awarded to my mother. They saw through my father – to their cost: he threatened the social worker so menacingly that, years later, a colleague of hers told me that she felt he had ruined her life.

However, my father's character-assassination of my mother in court was so effective that when my parents' divorce was granted early in 1985 my father was granted interim custody of me until permanent custody could be decided.

His smile was chilling on the day that he returned home from the court, came up to my bedroom where I was, and told me, 'I've got custody of you now.' But my mother told me, later on when he was out, that she hadn't given up. She was still fighting for custody and was determined to win.

This didn't cheer me at all, because I knew that either way the outcome would be equally bad. If he won I would be at his mercy, but if she did, he would pursue us both. So it meant very little to me whether he had custody or she did. I felt equally hopeless about it either way and my sense of impending doom deepened day by day.

Ironically, neither of my parents actually commented on the divorce itself. Although my mother had achieved what she had wanted for so long and this should have been a cause for celebration for her and for me, it wasn't. Their real focus was the custody battle, and presumably along with it the struggle for possession of the home, which continued long after the divorce was through.

The one real change was that after the divorce was granted they began living separately in the house. My father slept in the lounge while my mother had the bedroom – an arrangement which became the subject of yet another court hearing. My mother asked for the bedroom, but my father went in one evening and took it over. So my mother came and slept in my room until she could get the court to order that she should have their bedroom and my father must sleep downstairs.

They began keeping their food separately in the kitchen, splitting the fridge and the cupboards between them, and they never spoke to one another or spent any time in the same room, unless my father was launching yet another assault. Although my mother kept out of his way as much as possible, he still attacked her frequently, both verbally and physically.

Since my father had custody of me, he was responsible for feeding me. Sometimes he took me to Nan's or made me a meal, and at other times I just looked in his part of the fridge for something to eat. I noticed that in my mother's part of the fridge nice-looking ready-prepared meals and salads had started to appear. Like the new clothes, this was evidence of her growing independence and rejection of my father's oppression.

A few weeks after the divorce my mother came home one day and said, 'I've got custody of you now, Gayle.' Again, rather than feeling relieved, I felt very little emotion other than fear. I knew my father would never let her get away with it. But this was still temporary custody: the final battle for permanent custody was still to come. In the meantime my mother was now responsible for feeding me.

Now that they were living separately – even though they both remained under the same roof – any semblance of routine in the house had disappeared completely. Neither of my parents took any interest in me or seemed to have any expectations of me. I wasn't asked about my homework nor was I given any jobs to do and neither of them ever came to see how I was or to talk to me. I existed in my own lonely little world with only Sally, my doll, for company.

As the time approached for me to leave my primary school and go to secondary school, in the autumn of 1985, the battle between my parents raged over which school I would attend. My mother wanted me to go to a school close to home, but my father wanted me to go to another eight miles away, where he had connections and was friendly with several of the teachers. Once again I was petrified of being asked to choose. I told my mother that I wanted to go to the school she had chosen, and my father that I wanted his choice. I was drained by the effort of trying to show my mother that I loved her while trying not to inflame my father.

For some time I believed I would be going to my mother's choice of school, since she had custody of me. One day during the summer holidays Mum and I were walking into town discussing my new school. The next moment both of us suddenly stopped, looked at each other in alarm and then looked round. My father was following right behind us, eavesdropping on our conversation. He smiled at us, a slow, menacing smile, and even though he left soon we both fell silent for the rest of our outing. I felt he had deprived me of even this rare chance to enjoy my mother's company.

Both Mum and I were always hyper-vigilant, so I have no idea how we failed to notice that he was following us. It was as though he haunted us – he was never far away and I never felt free of his presence. He hated me talking to Mum and did everything he could to intimidate us and keep us apart.

The following day Louise came over for a while in the afternoon. I took her to my room to play and an hour or two later I went downstairs to get us both a drink. As I approached the bottom of the stairs I froze: even though I couldn't hear anything, I knew that something was happening in the kitchen. After a few seconds I walked into the room to find my father with his hands gripped tightly around my mother's neck. Mum was silent but her eyes were bulging and staring weirdly. I was terrified and felt powerless to do anything. Panicking, I walked past them and poured two glasses of squash.

At that point my father smashed his fist into my mother's mouth. Blood and tears streamed down her face. I wanted to stop him and protect her but I didn't know how. So I fled back upstairs with the drinks. A few moments later Louise looked out of the front window and saw my mother running down the road. Louise said, 'Your Mum doesn't have her handbag – why don't you run after her with it?' But I didn't answer Louise or run after my mother. I couldn't move – my body and my mind were numb, with no aware-ness of thoughts or feelings.

Louise said nothing more and shortly afterwards she

went home. I sat silently in my room for the rest of the evening. I didn't know where my mother had gone and I didn't hear her come back. The next day her face was so swollen and battered that I couldn't look at her without flinching.

Even though I know I was a child and hence powerless, to this day I still feel terrible guilt that I didn't do more to help her. I've gone over it in my head times beyond number, wishing that I could turn back the clock and find a way – any way – to save her from my father. If she had left him then, if I could have persuaded her to go, somehow, somewhere, then perhaps the terrible course of events that were now in train might have turned out differently. But I was so afraid of my father and so traumatised that I simply couldn't function in the face of his brutality. And my mother, over-optimistically given what we both knew about him, was still determined to find a way out for us through official channels.

Soon after this attack I was due to begin secondary school. But by that time my father had applied to the courts for a decision over which school I should attend and until the court hearing, a couple of weeks into the term, I had to wait. So I sat at home as all my friends began at school, not even knowing where I would be going for the next stage of my education.

My father won, and so two weeks late I started at Brock-hill Park Secondary Modern, eight miles – and a long bus journey – from home. I found moving schools very difficult.

I had been used to St Augustine's, but Brockhill was far bigger and I knew very few people – many of my classmates had gone to other schools. Thankfully, Louise was at Brockhill too, otherwise it would have been overwhelmingly awful. But even with her cheerful presence I felt very isolated from the other pupils, a loner, lost in my world of fear and sadness.

I felt very hopeless about life. I simply couldn't see a positive outcome for the battle raging between my parents. I couldn't imagine a situation in which either I or my mother might be happy and we might live in peace. My father was never going to let us get away, and I knew it.

I tried to avoid being at home as much as I could. If I came straight home on the bus from school I'd arrive back at 4.15 p.m. But in order to stay away I joined all kinds of after-school clubs and sometimes chose to walk the eight miles rather than taking the bus. Mostly I got back closer to seven in the evening. If I did get in earlier I would watch my favourite TV programme, *Grange Hill*, at 5.35 p.m. Otherwise I spent most of my time in my room.

I had got used to eating very little. I never had breakfast and I often spent my dinner money on confectionery on the way to school. By the time I got home I had often not eaten anything other than a few sweets or crisps all day. At that point there might be a meal, or there might not. Whoever had custody of me and was supposed to cook for me, there was no care taken over food and the meals – when they appeared at all – consisted of basic bland staples

such as sausage meat. I could perhaps have made something
to eat myself, except that very often there simply wasn't
any food in the kitchen. I didn't actually feel hungry very
often, because I was so deadened to all feelings other than
terror, and I was so used to eating very little. Although my
weight was low, it was not low enough to cause my teachers
any alarm – I had always been skinny.

By this time my father had won back temporary custody
of me. The final hearing was due to take place a few months
later, in July 1986. My mother had remained in the house,
not only in the hope of winning custody of me but also
of being given the right to stay in the family home. This
wasn't greed: she simply didn't have anywhere else to go
and hoped that, with me, she could make a new life for
herself there. But for that to happen my father would have
to leave. And while my mother might have hoped this would
be the outcome, I don't think it was something that my
father ever seriously envisaged. I would have loved for it
to have happened, but I didn't really imagine that it would.
It just didn't seem possible.

During the last year we all spent in the house together,
my mother was often in a bad way. Although she had her
job, and had tried so hard to make a new life for herself,
my father's frequent and violent attacks on her continued
and she still spent a lot of her time either in bed weeping
or crashing pots together in the kitchen. But now there was
another development. She had begun wandering around
the house whispering the word 'death' over and over again

to herself. I found this very frightening, I wanted to beg her to stop, but she didn't even see or hear me. Looking back, it's as if, despite her courageous stand, she sensed what was coming and in some way felt unable to stop it.

Meanwhile my father's preoccupation with Hitler had grown into an obsession and he quoted him extensively during the court hearings. He had chosen to represent himself throughout most of the proceedings – presumably considering that no lawyer would be up to the job. I was later told by someone who had been present that at one point the judge, completely exasperated, said to my father: 'May I remind you, Mr Sanders, that we're not here to talk about Hitler.'

At this point in my life I had a few friends of my own age, in addition to Louise, but very few adults who took any interest in me. The exception was my form tutor and head of year at school, Mrs Gilbertson, who was a warm, perceptive and sensitive woman who I came to feel was an ally. Of course I didn't tell her what was going on at home – I had never told anyone. And she didn't treat me any differently to any other pupil. But she was kind to me and that meant a great deal.

In February 1986 I turned twelve. Soon after my birthday came Mother's Day, and I was determined to do something special for my mother to try to cheer her up. I had saved up my pocket money for several weeks and I decided to buy her some flowers from the farmer who grew them in the school field. Mother's Day fell on a Sunday, so on the

Friday before the weekend I went across to the farm shop after school and carefully picked out a colourful bunch of delicate flowers that I thought Mum would like. But when I went to pay for them I didn't have enough money. The farmer took one look at my stricken expression and told me to take the flowers and forget about the rest of the money. Gratefully I took the bunch and carried it carefully home on the bus.

I couldn't hide the flowers until Sunday, so I gave them to Mum straight away. She thanked me, but I couldn't help feeling disappointed by the flatness of her tone and the apparent lack of pleasure she took in the gift. Although she managed a small smile, her eyes were dull and I felt she barely registered the flowers. As I sat in the kitchen and watched as she stood at the sink, putting them in a vase of water, I wished that I could have given her something to make her truly happy. But I knew that my mother's despair was so overwhelming that only freedom from my father – the one thing we both knew would be impossible to achieve – would lift it.

Four months later, on 29 July, the custody case was once again heard in Canterbury, at the County Court. This was the only occasion on which I was taken to court, and my father had prepared me well. If asked, I was to say that I wanted to live with him, he said. Did I understand that? I did.

In court His Honour Judge Sumner asked to see me in his chambers. 'Who do you want to live with?' he asked me. Obediently I said, 'My father.' The judge looked at me for a moment. Then he said, 'All young girls should live with their mothers' and took me back into court where he awarded permanent custody to my mother, with reasonable access granted to my father.

Far from feeling pleased, all I could think about was that my father would think I had disobeyed him. I was terrified. What I didn't know, until I saw the records many years later, was that my mother had found the courage to report my father for assault, and in an earlier hearing my father had given the court an undertaking not to repeat the offence. He had breached this undertaking by assaulting her again – and once again she had reported this. Why he wasn't jailed for breaching the undertaking I don't know. But what is certain is that my father's violent behaviour would have influenced the judge's decision over custody far more than anything I said. At the time, though, I knew nothing of this and feared that he would blame me.

My father lodged an immediate protest against the judgement and the case was referred to the Court of Appeal, which was due to hear it in November. Meanwhile, desperate to overturn the decision and win custody of me, my father's tactics became even dirtier.

One Friday afternoon my mother decided to take me to visit her parents. My father became incensed at this and refused to let us out of the house. While my mother and I stood in the hall, coats on and hand in hand, he stood with his leg across the door to prevent us leaving. He had the phone in his hand and was saying to the person on the other end – presumably the police or some official connected with the custody case – 'She's trying to take her away. Can I let her do it?'

He must have been told to let us go, because moments later he moved away from the door and we ran out.

A couple of hours later the doorbell rang at my grandparents' house. Two police officers stood outside and I felt a cold shiver of dread. 'We need to have a look at Gayle and see if she's all right,' one policeman told my mother and her startled parents. It seemed that my father had gone to the police and accused my mother of child abuse, telling them that she had beaten me. But I didn't know this until later; all I knew then was that the police had arrived and my grandmother was looking furious. I was certain I must have done something wrong and that the police arriving was my fault.

I was taken into the kitchen by my grandmother, and one of the policemen asked me to lift up my top so that he could see my tummy. I had no idea what was going on and I felt humiliated and frightened – and certain that my grandmother blamed me for the whole incident. I kept thinking 'What's happened?' but I didn't dare ask. Reluctantly I lifted my top a few inches while the policeman peered at my stomach and back and then said, 'That's fine, thank you.' He spoke briefly to Mum and then left with his colleague.

My mother and grandparents talked and they all looked

very angry. No one explained anything to me, and once again I was left feeling that no one cared in the least about how I felt.

Although they were now divorced and my mother had been given custody of me, my parents and I still remained in the house together. My mother, having come so far in her battle for independence from my father, had just one more hurdle to jump. She was waiting for the final verdict that she hoped would confirm her custody of me once and for all, and would also give her the right to keep the house. In this terrible atmosphere of accusation and counter-accusation, violence, intimidation and fear, we existed throughout that summer and into the autumn.

7

The day she died

The custody appeal was scheduled for Monday, 10 November. It had been made clear to me, both by my parents and by the Court Welfare Officer, that this would be the final hearing and there would be no more appeals. The absolute finality of this left me with a growing sense of hopelessness. I couldn't believe, for one second, that there would be a happy outcome and I went through the motions of life with a heavy sense of fatality about what the future would hold for us all.

The week before the hearing I went out to buy my mother a Christmas present. It was very early for Christmas shopping, but I was pleased because I had thought of the present I wanted for her. Knowing that she loved baths, I had decided to get her a big bottle of Boots's new pearly bubble bath. I was sure she would be pleased, and I took it home to hide in my room for the six weeks until Christmas.

In the few days before the hearing things felt eerily sinister at home. It was as though everyone in the house was waiting for something dreadful that we all knew was going to happen.

I slipped quietly out of the house to go to school and back in again at the end of the day, unnoticed. When my father wasn't being violent or abusive my parents avoided one another. But my mother was still muttering 'Death' and my father had taken to calling me into the lounge, where he sat in a chair in the dark. He made me stand in front of him while he talked in a slow, ominous voice about my mother and how she would not win the case. I was always frightened of the dark, and having my father force me to stand in the shadows and listen to him was so frightening that I can remember little of what he actually said.

At other times he looked pleased with himself, almost smug. I think he was so sure he would win the case and couldn't wait to gloat over my mother as he threw her out of the house, as he undoubtedly would.

The day before the court case my brother John and I had the only conversation I ever remember us having about what was going on between our parents. We talked about what would happen the next day and John, like me, was certain that things would not turn out well. He said, 'You do know that everything's going to change, don't you, Gayle?' and I nodded. We both did, and we both knew it would not be for the better.

I never felt the custody issue was truly about me. It was simply another battle between my parents, and I was their excuse. And I knew that, whoever won, the outcome would not be good.

On the morning of the hearing I didn't see either of my parents. I went into my mother's room where, as usual, she had laid out her clothes for the day. She was in the bath, so I knocked on the door, said goodbye and left for school.

Mum had arranged for me to go home with Louise after school and wait. Whoever won the case, she told me, would arrive to pick me up.

At Louise's house I was so numb with terror and anxiety that I could barely eat or play. I went through the motions of chatting to Louise while my fate was being decided in a court somewhere. I had no choice but to wait and see which of my parents arrived at the door to claim me. It was agonising. If Mum won I knew that my father would never let her get away with it. If he won, what would he do with me? And would he ever allow me to see my mother again?

After an hour or so the phone went, and Louise's mother came in to tell me that it had been my mother. She had won, and was on her way to collect me. Louise's Mum, assuming I would be pleased – though she knew nothing of what went on in our family – smiled at me and I struggled to smile back.

I should have been happy. Of course, in any normal circumstances I would rather my mother had custody of me than my father. But all I felt was a rising sense of panic. Something awful was going to happen, I was certain of that. I had been certain of it for months, but now the moment had come.

At about six in the evening the doorbell went. Mum came in smiling and said, 'I've got you something.' Then she handed me and Louise each a packet of Rolos – our favourite chocolate–and–toffee sweets. It was nice to see her looking happy, but I was surprised too. Wasn't she as scared as I was? Did she really think it would all be all right now? Or was she simply putting on a cheerful face to mask her fears? She appeared optimistic, but I felt the absolute opposite.

In a state of complete dread I heard Mum telling Louise's parents that we were going home. We were going to walk, but Louise's Dad offered to drive us. He got Mum's coat and held it while she put it on. It was a new one, long and greyish blue with a subtle pale grey stripe. Mum loved it and with her smart black heels she looked really nice in it.

As we drove the mile home Mum chatted to Louise's Dad. The radio was on and I remember that 'Take My Breath Away' by Berlin was playing.

We parked outside our house. The curtains were still open and no lights were on. Mum glanced at it and said, 'Thank goodness for that, he's not in.' Louise's Dad, perhaps in response to Mum's remark, and aware that there would be tensions after the court case, asked, 'Are you sure you're going to be OK? Do you want me to come in?'

Mum smiled at him. 'No, thank you, Peter, we'll be fine.' We got out of the car and waved goodbye as he drove off.

I have asked myself, as many others have asked me, why Mum went back to the house that night, knowing my father as she did. But no matter how many times I go over it, I simply don't know the answer. I was certain that we should not go back to the house and my heart sank as I watched Louise's Dad drive away. Yet my mother seemed to believe that it would be all right. Did she think that he would accept the verdict? Did she expect a beating, but believe it would stop at that? Did she believe he would go somewhere else for the night? I have no answers. But the events that followed are seared, in every last detail, into my memory. I have replayed them, in my despair and my grief, many thousands of times.

Mum turned and put her key in the door. But before she could turn it my father flung the door open from the inside. He had been lying in wait. He knew that my mother might not have gone in if she had known he was there, so he had waited, in darkness, to trap us.

His face was terrifying – his eyes were red and he looked possessed. As soon as she saw him Mum grabbed my arm and tried to pull me out of the house, so that we could run. But my father grabbed my other arm and tried to drag me inside. They both tugged so hard that I felt I was going to split in two.

Eventually my father managed to yank me into the house and my mother, still holding on to my other arm, stumbled in after me. My father grabbed at my front, picked me up by my coat, and literally threw me with all his might across the hall. I landed against the wall, at the bottom of the stairs. As I landed I hit my head on the wall. But I felt no pain – I was far too scared to notice.

I knew that we were both going to be killed. I watched as my father grabbed Mum and began punching her head from both sides, using first one fist and then the other. I saw her face being slammed from side to side as he hit her. Then he began punching her all over her body, raining blows on her stomach, head, legs and arms. She fell to the floor and he began kicking her, barely pausing between one vicious kick and the next. I sat crouched in the corner, watching, as my father dragged Mum by her hair out into the front garden. Her smart black shoes fell off, one after the other, and she called out, 'Gayle, please call the police!' She managed to say it three times before he climbed on top of her and began strangling her.

I knew she was begging me to save her life. In a panic I turned around, knowing that the phone was still padlocked, desperate for some way to help – and saw a noose made of orange cord on the floor. Beside it was another. As I stared at them I thought: he is going to hang me too. I looked out of the door towards my parents. My father was still on top of Mum. There was blood on her clothes and the grass, lots of blood. Her eyes were rolling, and at that moment she let out a high-pitched, painful and haunting scream. She managed to gasp just two words.

'You murderer.'

Those were to be my mother's last words, and they have haunted me since that day.

He dragged her back into the house, past me, and grabbed one of the nooses. I don't know if she was still conscious – she looked heavy and limp. He pulled her over to the stairs, put the rope around her neck and began tying the other end to the banisters.

As I watched, paralysed, I knew that he would come for me next. At that moment something changed inside me. I understood that I had to run – or die. It was a split-second choice. I snapped out of my paralysis and began to run.

I ran down the road to the nearest phone box and called Louise's house. As soon as the phone was picked up I said, 'Please come and get me, please come and get me now.' But the voice on the other end said, 'Sorry, you've got the wrong number.' In my panic I had got Louise's number wrong, and now I couldn't remember it at all. I threw down the phone and carried on running. I thought about going to Nan's house, as it was closest, but I knew I wouldn't be safe from my father there. So I headed for Louise's.

I kept looking over my shoulder for his car. I knew he would come after me. As I ran across the road I dropped the packet of Rolos, which had been in my hand all this time. I wanted to stop and pick them up, but I didn't dare.

I ran on, but kept looking back to the place where I had dropped the Rolos, desperate to have them.

When I got to Louise's door, her mother answered. Gasping for air, I said, 'My Dad's killed my Mum.'

Louise's mother looked startled, but said reassuringly, 'Don't worry, she's probably just fainted.'

Louise's family were having dinner. Her mother sat me down and went to talk to her father, who said he'd drive up and see if Mum was all right. But they had picked up on the urgency and distress I felt and before he went they phoned the police.

I sat in Louise's front room and kept saying, 'I want my Rolos, please take me back to get my Rolos.' Louise said, 'It's all right, you can have mine.' But I didn't want hers, I wanted mine. The ones that Mum had given me. Ever since then I've loved Rolos, because they remind me of my mother. Every time I go into a sweet shop, even now, I look for them.

It was Louise's Dad who found Mum hanging from the banisters in our house. There was no sign of my father, and the car was gone.

At Louise's house her sister Rachel phoned my sister at her boyfriend's. She and John had gone to court that day with our father.

I don't know how the two of them felt about my mother winning custody of me, but I have never blamed them for supporting my father, because I don't believe they had a choice. We were all controlled by him in one way or another.

Gran had gone to court that day too, to support Mum. Afterwards she had invited Mum back home with her, but Mum had said no, she wanted to collect me and go home.

Soon after Sarah got to Louise's, two policemen arrived at the door. They spoke to Louise's Mum and then took me and Sarah into the front room and sat us down. One of them said, in a very matter-of-fact way, 'I'm sorry but your Mum was pronounced dead in the ambulance.' Neither of us girls said a word. I had known that Mum must be dead, but hearing it from this stranger made it horribly real. I sat motionless, trying to take it in but unable to.

The policeman asked for the address of Mum's parents. Even in my state of shock I knew how hard it would hit them. I said, 'If Gran answers the door she'll be very upset – you mustn't tell her until they are together.' Later I heard that Gran did answer the door to the police, and as soon as she saw them she said, 'What has he done to her?'

My sister stayed at Louise's for a short while before leaving to go back to her boyfriend's. Apparently no one knew where my brother was. I imagine the police waited for him to get home and then told him. I don't know where he went that night.

The policemen went out to talk to Louise's mother and I heard one of them say, 'Can she stay here? There's nowhere else for her to go.' Louise's Mum said, yes, of course. But

I was puzzled. Why were the police asking friends to have me when I had family? Surely my grandparents or my uncle or aunt would be coming to collect me soon? I wondered which of them it would be, and who I would be living with now.

Louise's Mum sent us upstairs to prepare a bed for me in Louise's bedroom, and a few minutes later one of the policemen came up. He sat next to me on the bed and said, 'Can you tell me what happened?'

I said, 'I can't remember much. There was lots of blood and Mummy's eyes were rolling and she screamed "You murderer!" '

That was the whole of the police interview with me, the only witness to my mother's death. A brief chat, conducted in my friend's bedroom, only an hour or two after I had watched my mother being killed. They never spoke to me about it again.

A little later a doctor arrived. Without once looking me in the eye he passed me a pill and said, 'That will help you sleep.' Then he left.

A little later I asked Louise's Mum if Louise and I could stay off school the next day and she said yes.

At some point during the evening Louise's Dad came back. Finding my mother must have been an appalling experience for him. But he said very little, at least in front of me, and simply poured himself a large Scotch.

That night I slept, after taking the sedative that the doctor had left. It was only on the nights that followed that I lay in bed trying – and failing – not to think about the sight of my poor mother, or the terrible look on my father's face as he killed her, or the noose lying on the floor, waiting for me. And I tried not to think about her calling to me, and how I couldn't help her even though I so desperately wanted to. But I knew, even then, that those images would stay with me, every day, for the rest of my life. And I knew, too, that I would never, ever forgive myself for not being able to save her.

8

Numb with shock

The next day, as promised, Louise and I had the day off school. Louise's Mum took us for a walk, with the dog. Louise's mother was very kind to me, but I was completely numb and barely noticed anything that went on around me. All I could think was: 'What is going to happen to me?' I was in too much shock to take in what had happened, or the fact that my mother was gone.

Louise's parents didn't say anything to me about what had happened; they probably thought it best to try to be as normal as possible. But at some point I was told that my father was in custody and there would be a trial. I was relieved that he was locked up; now that I knew he really was capable of anything, my fear of him was even greater. I didn't know until much later that he had walked into a police station shortly after Mum died and said to them, 'I've done it, I've finally killed her.'

That afternoon Louise's Dad drove me back to our house so that I could collect some of my things. Louise came with us. When we arrived I thought I saw a cut-out image of my mother lying on the grass in front of our house, though I'm not sure whether I imagined it. Perhaps it was part of the police evidence. The house was the scene of a crime and must have been examined but, since my father had confessed, presumably the police didn't think it necessary to cordon it off. Louise and her Dad both came inside with me and he offered to come upstairs to my room but, embarrassed by the state of the house, I said no.

I had seen the night before that it was in disarray, but now I realised that my father had turned it completely upside down. The sofa and chairs were overturned and broken furniture, ripped-up books and smashed ornaments lay all over the place where he had thrown them. Not only that, but he had removed all the light bulbs, so that even if my mother and I had been able to reach a light switch the night before there would only have been darkness.

Now, in the sunless November light, the house felt spooky and cold.

Louise and I made our way quickly past the chaos on the ground floor and up the stairs from which, only hours earlier, my mother had been hanged. I didn't look at the banister, or think about what had happened. I focused instead on what I had to do.

I reached my room and looked around, uncertain about what I should take. Hastily I put a few randomly chosen clothes and my bunny pyjama case in a bag. In a drawer I found the bubble bath that I had bought Mum for

Christmas. I would never give it to her now, but I couldn't let myself think about that – I only knew that, somehow, I needed to have it with me. I put it in my bag and then went downstairs again, to where Louise's Dad was waiting. We all went out to the car and he drove us away while I sat in the back with Louise, staring straight ahead. The effort it had taken to get through the brief visit had been so enormous that I was beyond speaking or moving. It was only later that I realised I had forgotten Sally, my doll. I never saw her again.

The next day I went back to school. I didn't know it until later, but on the day I was away the teacher had told the class what had happened. They had found it so upsetting that one girl had had an asthma attack as a result. Unaware of this I walked in to curious looks and odd silences. Eventually a girl called Rebecca said, 'Hi, Gayle, I thought you might like a satsuma.' She was a sweet girl and I knew she was trying to make things better and acknowledge what had happened. I was grateful, because most people said nothing.

I simply went through the motions at school. I made my way from one lesson to the next and sat through classes, hearing nothing of what was being said. Mrs Gilbertson came and found me, put her arm round me, said how sorry she was and told me that I should come to her if I needed anything. Her kindness and her warm touch meant a great deal to me, but I felt unable to respond because I was far too desperate to know what was going to happen to me.

It may seem strange that I focused so completely on who would come to look after me. But the truth was that I was unable to grieve for my mother because I was in a profound state of shock, so profound that I didn't even have a sense of missing her. I was completely deadened to all feeling and could only think about who would take care of me, perhaps because it was my most urgent need at the time but also because it meant I didn't have to try to feel, or think about what had happened. It didn't even occur to me that there would be a funeral for Mum. I knew, of course, that someone who had died had to be buried, but I hadn't yet even been able to absorb properly the fact that she was dead.

This state of deep shock was to remain with me for several years, and throughout that time I was never really able to grieve. The need to survive overwhelmed everything else, and it was only much later that I was able to really feel the loss of my mother and acknowledge how enormously I missed her, and always would.

That first week no one in my family came to see me. Each night I lay in bed, wondering where they were and trying to imagine what it would be like to live with different family members. I went through my mother's family first. My Aunt Jane had three sons, and I mused whether she and her husband might like to have a girl as well. My Uncle David had a boy and a girl, and I wondered whether he and his wife would like a third child and whether my cousins would like me to move in. Then there were my grandparents; I asked myself whether they would like to have me, or whether they felt it would be a lot of work. If Gran and Grandad couldn't have me then perhaps Nan would. Or even my Uncle Ted, Dad's brother, whom I liked a lot.

My brother didn't visit me, but my sister did, briefly. She didn't say very much to me: we sat awkwardly in the lounge for a while before they got up and left. Neither my brother nor my sister knew how to cope with what had happened and they had no idea, any more than I did, where I would go. In our individual worlds, traumatised as we all were, we had never been able to talk to one another very much at home, and now we did not know how to convey our thoughts or feelings to one another.

The loss of our mother must have been terrible for Sarah and John, and I imagine they each coped in the best way they could. But there was one big difference between us. I had witnessed our mother's death and they had not. I knew exactly what had happened, and had seen the extent of our father's cold and calculating violence. For me there was no turning back. I had not been given a second-hand edited account. I knew. I had witnessed the unimaginable and this separated me from everyone around me. I would never, ever be the same again.

My brother was still living in our family home, along with his girlfriend, who had moved in with him. I was glad she was there. I imagined that it must be awful for him to remain in the house and I felt outraged that he had been

allowed to stay there at the age of only seventeen and wasn't
being looked after by an adult. He never told me how he
felt about it himself; there was so little said between us on
the few occasions when we met after Mum's death. As children we had never learned how to communicate, and after
our mother died it was too late to learn.

Just over a week after my mother's death my grandparents
came to Louise's house. They too said very little. They
certainly didn't mention me coming to live with them, or
even refer to what might happen to me. After they left my
anxiety levels rose even higher and, in an attempt to comfort
myself, I thought, 'Well, they're too upset to think about
whether they can take me right now, but perhaps they will
later.' Not that I felt it had to be them I lived with, I thought
it more likely that it would be my aunt or uncle, but more
than anything, I just wanted someone to want me.

I felt terribly conscious that Louise's parents were
having to look after me because there was no one else to
take me. I knew it wasn't right that they should do so
when I had a family of my own. But there was nothing
I could do.

I stayed with Louise's family for almost a month, and
during that time no one said anything about what would
happen to me, or what had happened to my mother. I knew
that she would have to be buried, but I had no idea when
her funeral would be, or when my father's trial would take
place. Day after day I waited for someone to arrive, put
their arms around me and say, 'Gayle, we'd like you to

come and live with us.' But no one did. And kind as Louise's parents were, they were in the dark too, also waiting to see what would happen. Doing their best in a very difficult situation, they tried to keep things as normal as possible. I've always been grateful to them for taking me in. Traumatised and desperate to know what would happen to me, I was glad of the safety and warmth of Louise's home, at least for that short while.

At one point Louise's Mum suggested, very gently, that I might like to move into the spare room. I'd been sleeping in Louise's room and her Mum probably felt that it would be sensible to give both of us a bit more space. Louise had been deeply affected by what had happened and had then had to cope with me, in my emotionally charged state, in her room.

I understood why her Mum asked me to move but I was deeply reluctant. Although I agreed to try it, I only lasted half an hour before I asked to go back to Louise's room. I couldn't articulate the fear I felt at being in a room on my own, and thankfully I didn't need to. I was moved back into Louise's room with no fuss and no further mention was made of the spare room.

Towards the end of my stay with Louise and her family a social worker arrived. Louise's Mum took me into the lounge to meet her and left us there together. The social worker introduced herself as Chris. Her manner was warm and friendly: she asked me how I was and then explained that I had been taken into care. I had no idea what that meant, but I didn't think to ask. Chris said that they were looking at the options for where I should live, and that I had been offered a temporary foster home with Mrs Briggs, the mother of my sister's boyfriend.

Again, I was puzzled – and very worried. Why would Mrs Briggs want me – and why didn't my own family? I wished that Chris would explain. Had all the members of my own family said they couldn't have me? Was that because they didn't want me? *Why* didn't they want me? The idea that people I loved had refused to have me was so painful. I felt alone, rejected and unloved, and was sure that they must all blame me for my mother's death. But I didn't ask Chris any of the many questions whirring round in my head, I simply muttered, 'OK.' At this stage – and for a long time afterwards – I was almost mute. I found it too difficult to put what I felt or thought into words and the longer this went on the harder I found it to speak. I was still paralysed by fear and I got so nervous that my mouth dried up and the words just would not come out. I struggled to talk, but it was beyond me. So I remained silent, and simply did as adults told me.

I knew Mrs Briggs, though not well. Her son Tim, Sarah's boyfriend, was nice, and Sarah spent a lot of time at their house. But my mother had hated Sarah going there, while my father, who was friends with Mrs Briggs, had encouraged it. I was horrified at the idea of being fostered by a woman whom my mother had clearly not liked, but again I said nothing. Of course, my sister was going to be there some of the time too, but it wouldn't be Sarah who would be responsible for me.

Later I would learn that both Sarah and John had been going to visit our father in prison every week. He had suggested to Sarah that she should apply for care and control of me and that I might go to live with Mrs Briggs until he came out of prison (he clearly didn't think he would be there long) and could take me back himself.

Interim care and control of me had been awarded to my sister on 5 December, twenty-five days after our mother's death. Meanwhile Sarah had asked for help from Mrs Briggs who, being a great friend of my father's and sympathetic to his plight – her view, as I was to discover, was that the 'poor man' had finally cracked, driven to what he did by that 'awful woman' – agreed to foster me. But as I listened to the social worker telling me that I was to go to the Briggs house, I knew that what she was really saying was that no one else wanted me.

That night I lay awake, trying to understand what was happening and why I was going to live with someone I didn't know. I blamed myself for my mother's death, and now I was sure that her family all blamed me too. Why else would they have left me for almost a month with no contact – apart from my grandparents' brief visit – and now be allowing me to go to a woman friendly with my father? My sense of loss, already profound, deepened. I realised that if I had thought, before my mother's death, that life couldn't get worse, I was now learning that it most certainly could. A whole lot worse. I hadn't just lost my mother, I had lost everything and everyone.

A few days later, along with my small suitcase holding all my possessions, I was collected by Chris and taken to Mrs Briggs's home. Louise's family all gave me a warm goodbye, saying they'd see me soon. I hoped so.

In Chris's car I sat in silence. Mrs Briggs lived not far from our old home, and the moment I stepped through her door I knew I didn't want to be there.

Mrs Briggs – I only ever called her by her formal title and she never invited me to do otherwise – was divorced and lived with her son Tim and daughter Maggie, who stayed from time to time. My sister stayed at her house some of the time, but was mostly away working. She had found a job in a school that offered accommodation, and came back to the Briggs household on her days off and at weekends.

From the outset I felt that Mrs Briggs didn't really like me or want me in her house. Her manner always seemed cold and unfriendly. When I arrived she showed me my room, told me to unpack and announced the time of dinner. No mention was made of my mother or what had happened. But in the following days it became clear to me that Mrs Briggs had no sympathy for me or my mother. She spoke to me very little other than to issue instructions, which I obeyed silently and woodenly. One day, when I revealed that I didn't know the name of a particular vegetable, she said, 'Your mother didn't bring you up very well, did she?' This wasn't the only time she pointed out the inadequacy of my mother's parenting.

I found this so painful that I could hardly bear to hear it. Although I didn't respond outwardly, inside I was in a turmoil. From the first time she criticised my mother I loathed Mrs Briggs and I decided that, although I had no choice about being in her house, I did have a choice about whether I ate anything while I was there, and I was certainly not going to eat her food. I would find a way, I decided, to avoid eating anything she had prepared. That would be my protest at her cruel and unjust criticisms of my mother.

Nine days after I arrived at Mrs Briggs's, on 19 December, my mother's funeral was held in the church in Dover which she had attended as a child and where she had sung in the choir. As in most cases of non-accidental death, it had not been possible to hold the funeral until some weeks after her passing because of the official procedures that had to be gone through.

A couple of days earlier, Sarah had told me about the funeral and had asked me if I wanted to go to the service in a big black car. This was the first mention of the ceremony – until then I'd had no idea when it would take place. I had asked her if we *had* to go in a black car, because then everybody would know what had happened. Sarah said no, we didn't have to, her boyfriend Tim could take us in his car. I was relieved, but there was another worry on my mind. I wanted to choose some flowers for my mother. However, no one asked me about flowers, and I simply didn't know how to ask.

On the day of the funeral Tim drove me, Sarah and John to the church. I sat in the car, thinking, 'Why is there no one with us and who is going to look after us? Someone should be looking after us.' I felt very strongly that someone in the family should be with us during our mother's funeral. But it seemed that we were on our own, not only in the car but when we arrived. I imagine this must have been as difficult for Sarah and John as it was for me. It was as though we were irrelevant, overlooked at our own mother's funeral.

We walked in together and took our places in the middle of a pew towards the back of the church. No one acknowledged us, let alone suggested that we sit at the front with the rest of our mother's family. As her children we should have been at the front, and I felt this very keenly at the time. In retrospect I have wondered whether the family may have behaved as they did because there was tension between our maternal grandparents and my brother and sister over my siblings' support for our father. But at such a time it was still wrong of them to disregard us.

None of my father's family were there. I think that even if they had wished to attend it would have been too painful for my mother's family to have them there.

Looking around I saw Mrs Wiggins, my teacher from St Augustine's with another teacher, Sister Matthew. I was surprised, and wondered who had told them, but so glad that they had come, to be there for my mother. Afterwards they came over to me and Mrs Wiggins put her arms around me – the only person who did so that day. They both gave me Christmas cards and later when I opened them I found that Mrs Wiggins's contained a five-pound Smith's voucher.

The local vicar who had known both my parents and had given so much support to my father had offered to conduct the service in his church. However, my grand-mother, feeling he had let my mother down, had refused to let him have anything to do with it, which is why the service was being held at the church that my mother had attended when she was a little girl.

The service was plain and short. There was no eulogy in which my mother was remembered or paid tribute. A couple of prayers and a couple of hymns and it was all over. My sister sat holding hands with Tim, but John and I had no one and again I thought, 'Why isn't one of our relatives with us? Someone should be looking after us.' Up at the front of the church I saw Grandad, his shoulders heaving as he wept, Gran's arm around him.

I didn't cry. I couldn't because I was frozen. I had shut down completely and was able only to put one foot in front of the other, and do as I was told.

After the service the four of us went back to Tim's car to drive to the crematorium. I didn't understand what cremation meant. I thought that when people died they were put into a coffin and buried in the ground. I had vivid images of my mother being nailed to a cross and set on fire, while we had to watch her burn. No one told me anything about it, and I couldn't ask.

By the time we got to the crematorium I was terrified. I had already seen my mother die – I couldn't watch her body being burned. I told the others I couldn't come in, so they said I could sit in the car on my own.

After the service my grandmother came out to get me and said, 'Come on, come and look at the flowers.' So I went with her to have a look. As we approached I saw there was some kind of disturbance going on, and when we reached the flowers I saw why. The biggest, grandest bouquet was from my father.

I felt sick. Anything that reminded me of my father sent me into a state of complete terror. Even though I knew he was in prison, I was absolutely certain that he was still after me, still watching me, and would get me in the end. Clearly everyone around me felt horrified at his bizarre gesture in sending over-the-top flowers to the wife he had just killed. I did too, but for me they were also a sinister reminder that he hadn't gone away – and would be back.

I turned and went back to the car. Minutes later Sarah, Tim and John came back to the car and we went back to my grandparents' house, where there was a small wake. It was very low-key, only a handful of people, and I sat at the side of the room, ignored for most of the time. The only person who spoke to me was my mother's brother, Uncle David, who went out of his way to come and say hello.

Soon after the funeral I received a small package through the post. Inside was a bottle of Rive Gauche perfume and a letter, which said: 'You do not know me, but I am in love with your father and I will wait for him. Perhaps we can all live together when he is free.'

It was clearly not from the nurse in Essex, but someone else. I was horrified, not so much by this clear evidence that he had been involved with this woman as by the fact that he must have given her my address and allowed – or even encouraged – her to write to me. I found her letter bizarre and insensitive. I threw the perfume and the letter away and never told anyone about them. But I couldn't forget them, not the reminder they contained that my father intended to reclaim me once he was out of prison.

Christmas was only six days after my mother's funeral. No relative invited me to be with them, so I had no choice but to spend the day with Mrs Briggs. Sarah was there too, with Tim, but I was there only because there was nowhere else to go.

Just before Christmas a man had arrived at the door asking for me. 'This is from your Dad, in prison,' he had said, handing me a small parcel. Inside was a pair of long red socks. I felt this was simply my father's way of saying 'I'm still here, I know where you are, and I will be coming for you.' Shaking and feeling nauseous, I threw them in the bin.

John was still living with his girlfriend in our old house. Although he was only seventeen, social services had decided that he could manage and had agreed to let him stay there. I wondered if it was hard for him, being in the house where Mum had died. It seemed to me quite wrong that he had been left there but, even so, there were moments when I felt I would rather manage there than be at Mrs Briggs's.

She continued to run my mother down, so I carried through my plan not to eat any of her food. It was the only way I had of keeping some little corner of my spirit alive. I refused to let her crush me. I had never been a big eater, and had never been used to regular meals, so I found her insistence that I eat breakfast very difficult. I soon found a way round it, by coming down early in the morning, putting a few cornflakes and a spoon of milk into a bowl, and telling Mrs Briggs, when she appeared, that I had already eaten. On the way to school I would spend my dinner money on sweets – I loved pineapple chunks and cola cubes – or crisps and a can of fizzy drink, as I always had.

In the evening Mrs Briggs prepared dinner, which we ate in the lounge on our laps. I would toy with mine until she'd finished hers and went out to feed her cats. Then I would scoop my food into a plastic bag that I had ready, and shove the bag into my pocket until I could dispose of it in the dustbin or, failing that, on the way to school the next day.

Most of the time Mrs Briggs and I were on our own. Her children were young adults and were out a lot. And when my sister came to stay I barely saw her: she and Tim went out together and we never exchanged more than a few words before she'd be off to her job again. We had never been close, and these painful circumstances did not bring us closer.

In fact, I think there were many undercurrents in the family that I, as a child, was not aware of, and what happened to me after my mother's death was a result of these. Because of Sarah and John's support for my father – both before and after the killing – my mother's parents were very cold towards them and had very little to do with them for some time. Perhaps, because of my older siblings and the letters my father had forced me to write, attacking my mother, they thought that I too supported our father and this was what caused them, and my aunt and uncle, to distance themselves from me. If so, they could not have been more wrong. I hoped fervently that I would never have to see my father again. I could not get out of my mind the picture of his face as he killed my mother, or her desperate cries for me to get help. I replayed the scene over and over, hearing her begging me to get help and trying to think of how I could – and should – have saved her.

I did see family members, a handful of times, while I was at Mrs Briggs's. Nan, my father's mother, lived a half-hour walk away and one day I went to see her after school. I didn't blame her for what had happened, and I wanted to keep in touch. Neither of us mentioned anything to do with my mother's death. She seemed a little sad and I felt very tense: we both knew that things would never be quite the same again. But we had tea and Nan chatted to me and gave me chocolate and apples, which I was grateful for. And when I left she asked me to come again, and I did, several times. In a way I felt sorry for her. Her son was a killer and I knew that must have been very hard for her.

On a handful of occasions I was allowed to go and stay with Gran and Grandad overnight. Once again, nothing was said about what had happened, and we all tried hard to behave normally. I told them I didn't like Mrs Briggs, or the food she gave me, so Gran would give me some food to take back with me – usually just a piece of one of her home-made cakes, in a small plastic bag. They would drop me outside Mrs Briggs's door and when she saw the bag she would say sarcastically, 'Oh, I see they've given you a doggy bag.'

I was still hoping that my grandparents, aunt or uncle might take me to live with them. Mostly I didn't say anything, but on one occasion, when I was with my Aunt Jane, I plucked up all my courage and said: 'Could I come and live with you? Don't you think it would be nice to have a girl? I'd be so good, I promise.'

Jane looked away. 'I'm sorry, Gayle, I've got my own boys to look after,' she said. My sense of rejection was absolute, but even as I ached with the hurt of it I respected her for giving me a direct answer and being honest with me. At this point, the reality that nobody in the family was going to take care of me was beginning to sink in. It confirmed what I had always believed: that I was not lovable, and I began to think about suicide.

Many years later, in a rare reference to my mother's death, my grandmother said to me, 'Nobody in the family did anything for you because they were all so traumatised.' It was an acknowledgement — the first I had ever had — that I had been abandoned by the family. But was it simply because they were traumatised? Or was I somehow, in their minds, associated for ever with her death because I had witnessed it? Whatever the truth, in my twelve-year-old mind there was only one reason why no one wanted me. They all believed, as I did myself, that I was to blame for my mother's death.

9

Sinking into despair

Living at Mrs Briggs's place in the absence, as I in my distressed state perceived it, of kindness, affection or warmth, my condition declined. I had never been a good sleeper, but now I had become terrified of the dark and had to keep the lights on at night. Even then I couldn't sleep, and when I finally did I suffered appalling nightmares that left me trembling and wide awake for the rest of the night.

I was also still eating very little and had lost weight. I didn't care about food, or anything else. I was seriously depressed and simply couldn't see the point of being alive any more.

Mrs Briggs was unaware of my unhappiness – I kept it hidden from her – and life in her house became increasingly difficult for me. One day she shouted at me for using too much toilet paper. Rather than risk her wrath again, I decided I would stop using the toilet in her house. From then on I waited until I got to school each day. Desperate to pee, and to avoid her, I began leaving the house very early in the morning, when Mrs Briggs was still in bed. No matter how torturous it was, it gave me some small sense of satisfaction to know that I had managed to avoid using that loathed woman's toilet.

Inevitably my disturbed state began to show at school. By early 1987, two or three months after my mother's death, I was feeling actively suicidal. I would sit in class writing the word 'death' over and over again on the exercise book in front of me. The girl who used to sit next to me, Andrea, had become a friend and was sympathetic about me having to live with Mrs Briggs, but she became upset by my fixation with writing 'death' and asked me to stop. I felt bad for upsetting her and apologised. But I couldn't stop myself from writing the word which dominated all my thoughts and I went to sit at the back of the class so that I wouldn't upset Andrea.

Mrs Gilbertson kept an eye on me. She was, at this stage of my life, the only person who ever put an arm around me. She didn't ask me any questions, she simply gave me a hug whenever she could. She probably had no idea just how much that simple gesture meant to a child who was so utterly starved of any kind of affection and who felt so very unwanted. She wasn't afraid to touch me, when I felt that almost everyone else was.

Almost every day I would go to Mrs Gilbertson, say I had a headache and ask if I could go to see the school secretary. She would say yes, and I would go and sit with the secretary in her office. She was a pleasant woman who didn't mind me sitting beside her for a couple of hours each day while she carried on with her work. We said very little, but that was fine with me. I preferred sitting with her to struggling through my lessons, so I would stay for as long as I could, until she suggested that perhaps, if I was feeling better, I might like to go back to my class.

Most of the time I said very little to anyone. But on a few occasions I found it impossible to contain my feelings any longer. One of those times was in a science lesson when a girl sneered at me, 'You're having sex with your Dad.' I have no idea why she said it – she couldn't have known that I had indeed been a victim of sexual abuse because I had never told anyone. But her taunting hit a raw nerve and I crawled under the desk, curled myself into a tight ball and began rocking back and forth, trying to squeeze her words out of my head.

The teacher in charge of the class, alerted by the other children, went to get Mrs Gilbertson, who came and, taking my hand, led me gently out of the room. Although I was walking, I was still bent over almost double and I was breathing so rapidly that I could barely draw the next breath. Mrs Gilbertson took me into her office, put her arms around me and cuddled me. Eventually I was able – still gasping and struggling to get the words out – to tell her what had happened.

'I'm so sorry, Gayle,' she said. 'But what the girl said is not true, is it?' It had taken every ounce of energy I could muster to tell her. I wanted to say more, to tell her that it was, in a way, true. But I couldn't. I simply nodded, which she took as my confirmation that she was right.

It wasn't unusual for me to walk around in a hunched-over position, my head hung so low that I was looking down at the ground. On another occasion I arrived for a science lesson late, bent almost double. The teacher told me to go out and come in again properly. I hated her for singling me out when all I wanted was to slide in unnoticed. To be made the focus of attention was awful. I looked at her and said, 'No, I'm going to go and never come back and you'll never see me again.' I walked out of the class and out of the school building, and went to sit in the playing field. All I could think about was what it would be like to jump in front of a train. I wanted everything to end, I wanted to escape the unbearable misery of my life, and that was the best way I could think of to do it.

I sat there for some time, and then remembered that the next class was PE, which I liked. I decided to go back, and I was in the changing rooms getting ready for the lesson when Mrs Gilbertson came in. I had my top off and felt embarrassed, holding it to my front as she approached me. Mrs Gilbertson wasn't often angry with me, but I could see both anger and fear in her expression as she said, 'Don't ever do that to me again.' I realised that she must have been looking for me, frightened that I had left the school and perhaps harmed myself.

*   *   *

On 17 February 1987, just over three months after Mum's death, my father was committed to appear at Canterbury Crown Court. At around the same time Mrs Briggs and my sister had me made a Ward of Court. This meant that the court would have the ultimate say over what happened to me. I was certain that my father had instructed them to do it – he would make sure that in any decision-making process the court heard his views, and in this way would continue to play a part in controlling what happened to me.

A few days later, on 26 February, I turned thirteen. My Uncle Ted, my father's brother, had invited me to stay and I was surprised and pleased. Although I had been on my own to visit Nan a few times, on the way home from school, I had only seen Ted's family once in the three and a half months since Mum's death and I had never stayed with them before.

I liked being at their house; it was calm and felt comfortable there. Ted took me to a dry ski slope for my birthday treat and I slept in their grown-up daughter's bedroom. They let me eat whatever food I liked and I was surprised by how early they went to bed, though I didn't mind.

Although I appreciated their kindness, I was still in a daze and felt very distant. I don't know how much this showed – I made an effort to join in and the few days I spent with them were so much nicer than being with Mrs Briggs. But sadly this was to be one of the last times I would see the family: a few months later I was removed from all contact with anyone I knew.

During the time I was at Mrs Briggs's place I was still being visited by Chris, my social worker. I had also been sent several times to see a psychiatrist, Dr Hayter, a tall, thin woman who always wore skirts. I could see that she was concerned about me, but I was unable to talk to her about what had happened, any more than I could talk to anyone else. We sat without speaking throughout most of each fifty-minute session, the silence broken only by her occasional questions and by the sound of her stomach rumbling. I was a lost child, so traumatised that I could barely function, and as I was totally unable to open up I don't think she felt she was helping. I did actually like her, but I didn't know where to start. How could I, when I was locked inside my own world full of troubling thoughts and memories? In hindsight, I think it would have been helpful to have been given play or art therapy. I might have been able to express, in a creative way, some of the feelings I couldn't put into words.

My social-services notes of that time describe me as: 'Severely traumatised and suffering from recurrent night-mares. A very confused and unsure child who feels guilty about her mother's death, believing that if she had called for help sooner she might have prevented it.' That was part of the story, and it was certainly bad enough. But what the notes don't say is how petrified I was of my father, and how my fear of being returned to him dominated my every waking hour.

Chris and Dr Hayter asked me if I wanted to visit my father while he was in prison on remand. I think they both had reservations about it, but he had been repeatedly making requests for me to visit him and they felt that they had to check it out with me. Seeing him again was actually unimaginable. I dreaded and loathed the idea – it kept me awake night after night. But at that time I was a child in a state of severe shock and simply did what the people around me assumed I would do. Most significantly, perhaps, I knew that my father expected it, and even at a distance I was still controlled by him in that I was conditioned to do what I knew he wanted.

There was one other aspect of the situation, too. Although I hated the idea of being anywhere near my father, I felt that in some strange way I needed to go and see for myself that he was truly behind bars, locked away and unable to get out or to get to me. So, reluctantly, I agreed.

We set off on the appointed day, travelling by car. Chris and Dr Hayter were in the front, while I sat, rigid and silent, in the back. We had to park outside the prison and walk through the entrance, and as we went through the huge metal gates my whole body tensed with fear. More than anything I wanted this visit to be over.

The guard indicated that we could walk through. The prison was enormous and intimidating, its grey walls towering above my head. Inside the visiting area Chris and Dr Hayter had their handbags checked and we were all body-searched, a woman officer tapping me all over, which

I found horribly intrusive and didn't understand. No one had thought to explain to me that I would be searched, or why.

Another officer came to take us to see my father. He smiled over his shoulder. 'Your Dad's a great guy,' he said. 'He's really looking forward to seeing you.'

So he's won you over, too, I thought. But I didn't say anything. I felt numb and disconnected, almost as if I wasn't really there. And, in truth, I think a part of me wasn't there. The part of me that had died with my mother that day.

We were led into a cold, claustrophobic little room that had a tiny barred window in the top corner of one wall. There were a table and a couple of chairs, and we were asked to wait. It was grim – no place for a child. And yet the prison officer was smiling at me, as if I should somehow be pleased or even excited.

I knew my face was set and expressionless. All I could do was stare ahead as the dread inside me grew with every passing second.

As my father was led into the cell he tripped slightly, but quickly steadied himself. He saw me and walked straight over, enveloping me in a hug. I was rigid as he pulled me onto his lap. I sat there like a little statue, staring out of the tiny window in the top of the wall, as he chatted cheerfully about the awful food, and the plastic slippers that he had to wear. He asked what I was doing at school and I managed to mumble 'Nothing much.' I think those were the only words I spoke.

My discomfort was enormous. I felt humiliated that Chris and Dr Hayter were seeing my father put his arms around me. I was afraid they would think I wanted him to do it and I felt desperate to stop him, although I was completely unable to and sat passively without moving.

The visit seemed unending, but eventually my father was led out of the room and the guard took us back to the entrance. When we got outside the prison I turned to Chris and Dr Hayter.

'I don't want to go back there,' I said. 'I don't ever want to see my father again.'

Seeing him had been a huge mistake. His false sincerity, his attempt to convince me as well as Dr Hayter and Chris that he cared for me, and the way he had already won over the guard, all sent me into a worse spiral of fear and depression. More than ever, I truly wanted to die.

Chris and Dr Hayter realised that the visit hadn't been a good idea, and it was never again suggested that I should go. In fact, they were among the few people who distrusted my father: Chris made it clear to the other authorities involved in my care that she didn't feel any further contact with him was helpful or desirable.

It wasn't often that people, even professionals, saw through my father. The psychiatrist who later testified at his trial found him to be a perfectly reasonable man. But every now and then someone saw him for what he was. It was long after he left prison that I learned another psychiatrist had described him as 'a psychopath with a plausible-personality disorder'. In other words, a psychopath, deranged and with no conscience whatsoever, who was able to mimic a completely normal and plausible personality. It fitted perfectly with the monster I had witnessed at home, so charming to outsiders, so terrifyingly cruel behind closed doors.

Chris was never taken in by my father. She saw him for what he was from the beginning. It took me a long time to come to trust Chris, and to see that she was on my side, but in time I did. She was always straight with me, which I appreciated. So many people patronised me, or assumed things about me, but Chris never did. She just waited patiently for me to talk and accepted it if I didn't want to.

It was by this time clear to social services that the arrangement with Mrs Briggs would not work in the long term. She was no doubt feeling out of her depth in coping with me and was reporting to them that I was uncooperative and wasn't eating, while I had told Mrs Gilbertson and Chris that I was not happy. Over the next few months social services did their best to find me a more suitable foster home. However, nothing could be found unless I moved schools to another area and that was not considered to be a good idea. I had said I wanted to stay at the school, as it was the one constant in my life, and the one place I felt reasonably safe.

With hindsight I think this was a mistake. I believe I should have been sent to a foster family who specialised in helping children in trauma, and moved right outside the area so that I could make a fresh start, away from people who knew or were involved with my father. I know that social services did their best. And a lot more is known now about how to help traumatised children. Leaving me in contact with so many people who were in touch with my father only added to my trauma. But at the time no one really understood that.

So I continued to wait – but with little hope – for someone to want me, for some kind of permanence, for a future. I spent hours thinking about killing myself. I planned to jump in front of a train or from a cliff. These seemed to me the most certain ways of dying. And although the prospect of killing myself was daunting, I wasn't afraid of death itself nearly as much as I feared what lay ahead for me in life.

One day at school Mrs Gilbertson took me to one side and said, 'There's something I need to tell you, Gayle.' In her office she told me gently that my father had, earlier that day, been sentenced to three years in prison. It was 8 May, which also happened to be his birthday.

'I know that seems a long time, but it isn't, really,' Mrs Glbertson said soothingly. I looked at her. Did she, like so many others, think he was a decent man who had made a 'mistake'? Or did she say this for my benefit, believing that I would be shocked and upset that my father was to remain in prison at all. I couldn't find the words to say that my shock was at how *short* the sentence was. All I could think was, 'He got away with it.' I knew that with the time he had already served on remand, he would be free very soon.

Mrs Gilbertson suggested that I might like to go to her house for the night. This certainly hadn't been planned and I imagine that Mrs Briggs had asked her to do it. Perhaps she didn't feel up to coping with my reaction to the brevity of my father's sentence, though by now she should have known that, whatever I might feel, I would say little or nothing. Another rejection, or the perception of one, coming after so many others hurt me, even though I didn't like Mrs Briggs. But I was happy at the thought of staying with Mrs Gilbertson.

I was never given any details of my father's trial. It was only years later that I was able to find out what I had already suspected. He was allowed to plead guilty to manslaughter on the grounds of diminished responsibility. During the trial he brought into court people who were seen as pillars of the community to be his referees, and to tell the court what a marvellous, caring man he was and how totally out of character his actions had been.

These character witnesses included the local vicar, who told the court that my father had taken the decision to train for the clergy and would himself be a minister eventually.

My mother's killing was regarded almost universally, it seemed, as 'an unfortunate accident'. My father told the court that he had intended to kill himself and only at the last moment, in his grief at being deprived of his child, had killed his wife instead. No one, apparently, realised that he had prepared a second noose, and therefore – even if he had planned to kill himself, which I don't for one second believe to be true – he had clearly intended to kill someone else too.

How he must have smiled to himself at the sheer blind folly of all those who smiled and patted him on the back and told him that he didn't really deserve to be locked up at all, but never mind, with good behaviour he could be out in a year.

I felt that my mother had been utterly betrayed by all those people who had testified for my father. Most of all I felt that the vicar had broken faith with her, because she had gone to him for help. I later heard that my grandmother felt the same way – and she wrote to the Archbishop of Canterbury in protest at the vicar's testimony.

The vicar's congregation also objected to his support for my father, it seemed, because after the court case many of them boycotted the church. I was glad when I heard this, but I couldn't help thinking, 'Where were you all when my mother needed help?' It was all very well protesting, and at least it showed that not everyone thought my father was a great guy who'd made a tragic error. But nothing was going to bring my mother back.

I did hear that the vicar eventually expressed regret for the level of support that he had given my father. He realised his error, but too late: by that time he had helped to win my father a pathetically short sentence.

No one had even asked me – the only witness to my mother's death – what had really happened. Apart from the three-minute police 'interview' in Louise's bedroom on the night my mother died, I had never been asked anything about it.

Twenty-two years on, things would be done very differently, and I'm glad of that. Today, a child in the same position would be given a great deal more care and support, and would be interviewed in an appropriate setting by fully trained specialist police officers. Had that been available to me, I might have told them not only what had really happened but what had been going on in our house all my life. As it was, I appeared to be considered irrelevant to the entire case.

After the trial things were set in motion to sell the family home – John would then move into a flat of his own and the proceeds would be split between Sarah, John and me. My share was to be put into trust, for me to have when I reached the age of eighteen.

At Mrs Gilbertson's I was grateful to be away, even if only for a short while, from Mrs Briggs. For one night at least I wouldn't have to hear her sing my father's praises and denigrate my mother yet again.

Mrs Gilbertson and her husband were kind and thoughtful. They lived in the country and we went for a walk and I helped Mrs Gilbertson cook. But, distressed by how short my father's sentence was and consumed with the fear that he would soon be able to claim me, I was unable to relax or enjoy being with them. And, to compound my discomfort, when I went to bed Mrs Gilbertson asked for my clothes so that she could wash them for the next day. I felt terribly embarrassed – I was so intensely private that I couldn't bear to think of her doing something as intimate as washing my clothes.

The next day I went to school with Mrs Gilbertson and then returned to Mrs Briggs's in the afternoon. No one at her house, including my sister, mentioned the court case at all.

A month later, on a Friday afternoon in June, I arrived back from school to find my room bare. All my possessions had gone. I ran down and asked Mrs Briggs where my things were. She told me that she had packed them because I was leaving.

I was almost more upset about her invasion of the little privacy I had than I was at the prospect of moving to somewhere I had not even been told about. I didn't have many belongings and none of them were especially personal, but they were all I had. To find that Mrs Briggs had put them into a bin liner felt like a violation of my being.

Where was I going? And why hadn't I been given any warning? I sat on my bare bed and waited until Chris arrived to collect me. She explained that they had been unable to find me a suitable foster home and felt that I needed some more specialist help, so she was taking me to a kind of hospital where I would be looked after.

I sat silently in the car, scared of the unknown and

wondering what this place I was being taken to was. After half an hour we turned up a long driveway, and Chris told me this was the St Augustine's psychiatric hospital in Chartham. I'm sure she didn't know it, but this was the same place to which my mother had once been taken by my father.

My first impression was of grass and trees as we drove through the grounds to the main hospital building. From there we continued along the small access road to the adolescent unit, Beech House, which was several minutes beyond the main building.

Inside I was taken to a small room where I was greeted by two people I presume were doctors. 'Gayle, we think you need a bit of help,' they said. 'And this is a place where we help children.'

I hated their patronising tone. 'I don't want to come here,' I told them. But it was quite clear that I had no choice. I was asked to sign the papers agreeing to be admitted.

'If you don't come voluntarily, then we will have to force you,' they said. Just like my father, I thought, forcing me to sign something I don't agree with. But then, where else was I to go? No one wanted me, not even a foster family. Was this really my only option? And what about school – until now they had considered it important for me to stay at the same school, but now I realised even that was to be taken away from me. They explained that I would go to the hospital's own school, but I was distraught.

I am sure that the decision to put me in St Augustine's was taken in the belief that it would help me. My social-services notes of the time shed a little more light. 'Gayle's increasing depression gives rise for great concern,' they state. 'Mrs Gilbertson says Gayle is just coping, but comes into school almost daily with severe headaches. She has talked to Mrs Gilbertson of wanting to end things.'

Clearly social services felt I was in such a bad way that the chief criterion applied to my care so far – keeping me at the same school – was no longer appropriate in the circumstances. However, taking me away from everyone I knew and isolating me in this place would only make me more insecure, unsafe and unable to open up. What I needed was to feel safe, in a caring family, where I could begin to build up trust. But that didn't seem to be an option, so here I was, in a soulless, loveless institution.

I hated the look and feel of the place. Despite the beautiful grounds surrounding it, inside it was ugly and the endless corridors, wards and offices sent a chill through me. The place was dirty, run-down and ugly. There were bolts on all the doors and windows and there had been no attempt to make it homely or inviting. Everything seemed clinical and impersonal.

Horrified that I was to be locked away in this place, away from Mrs Gilbertson, Louise and my other school friends, I felt the only option left to me was to kill myself.

I told the doctors and Chris that I wanted to go to the school disco that evening. They agreed that I could, as long as I was admitted to the hospital the next morning. The disco was to be held at a community centre called The Pavilion, which was on a hillside and looked down on a steep drop to the road below. It would provide me with an opportunity.

That evening at the disco, I went out across the patio to the railings which formed the barrier around the perimeter. I looked down to the trees lining the roadside, the road beyond and, on the other side of it, the sea. It was a long drop. Long enough, I was sure, to kill me.

I climbed over the railings and stood on the other side, preparing myself. At that moment a girl I knew appeared and asked me what I was doing. I told her I was going to jump and said goodbye. But she climbed over next to me, put her hand on my arm and said, 'If you jump, I'll jump too.' We weren't close friends at all, but she must have cared and intuitively she said the right thing to stop me. I knew I couldn't be responsible for her death and reluctantly I climbed back over the railings and went with her into the disco.

That night I went back to Mrs Briggs's for the last time, and the next morning Mrs Gilbertson – who must have volunteered for the task – arrived to drive me back to Beech House. As I was shown to my bare little room I felt sure I couldn't survive here.

I said goodbye to Mrs Gilbertson and watched her drive away. At that moment I knew I had lost everything. My last remaining lifelines – school, Louise and her family, and

Mrs Gilbertson – were being taken away from me. Even Chris, my social worker, whom I was just beginning to like and trust, was taking a back seat and would only visit very occasionally as care of me was now handed over entirely to the hospital.

As I sat on the hard little metal-framed bed, I decided that my father must have convinced the court that it was really me who had killed my mother. Why else would they be locking me up in this terrible place?

10

Hospital

My first impression of the psychiatric hospital was soon confirmed. I found the adolescent unit a bleak, dull and sad place where no children – let alone troubled and unhappy ones – should have been housed. Most of the twelve or so kids were in there because of behavioural problems – several had dropped out of school or had been violent. Most of them seemed very loud and street-wise, while I was quite the opposite. At just thirteen I was the youngest teenager there, and I was certainly the quietest. Most of the others were in their mid or late teens, and as I looked younger than I actually was the gap between me and the rest of them appeared even bigger than it actually was. But despite this they were friendly to me – although I wasn't very interested in responding. I didn't want to be there and I didn't want to have to make friends.

The others all talked, at times, about their parents and families. Not all of what they said was positive, but most of them received regular family visits and went home for occasional weekends. I was the only one with nowhere to go, and there were times when I was the only patient left in the unit. I was also one of only two patients with no visitors. I had agreed to the doctor's suggestion that I shouldn't see anyone I knew for a while, as they felt it might make it easier for me to open up. But in fact all it did was to isolate me further and this exclusion only reinforced how completely unwanted I felt. Within a few weeks I was convinced that everyone who ever knew me had simply forgotten me and that, while I missed them, they didn't miss me at all.

Every day we followed the same routine. We got up at seven-thirty, washed and made our beds. Our wake-up call was Whitney Houston's 'I wanna dance with somebody'; one of the girls on the unit loved it and she played it at top volume, morning after morning. I liked the song and hearing it in the mornings provided some sense of normality in the unit. After that we had breakfast in the dining room – or at least the others did, because I didn't want to eat, and the ghastly food there meant that I managed to swallow even less than I might otherwise have. I just sat and toyed with a piece of toast or a bowl of cereal.

After breakfast we all had to go to the group room, where we sat in a circle – patients and staff – and, one by one, had to say what the day before had been like for us. The staff insisted that all of us teenagers had to say something and I absolutely hated it. I resented being forced to talk and felt it was pointless. What kind of day did they *think* we'd had, in this awful place? As my turn approached my mouth became increasingly dry and my breathing more and more shallow. When my turn came and all the heads in the room turned in my direction, I spoke two brief sentences: 'My day yesterday was OK. That's all I have to say.' I repeated this, word for word, every single day.

We also used to have 'open' therapy sessions in which we were encouraged to talk about our feelings. I hated these encounter groups too, because I felt under pressure to do what was impossible for me. Once a month or so they took the form of psychodrama, in which we were encouraged to act out our feelings. I found these gatherings almost laughable. We would be taken into a carpeted room – and when I say carpeted I don't just mean the floor: there was carpet covering all the walls, too – and were encouraged to 'get angry'. They told us stories to provoke us and gave us rolled-up newspapers to hit cushions with. I couldn't do it: the whole thing just made me cringe. They would say to me, 'Gayle, you should be angry,' and once they even threatened to throw a bucket of water over me in an effort to rouse the furious feelings that they were convinced were ready to explode out of me. Nothing they did worked. I felt the whole thing was chaotic, badly managed and pointless.

There was a school attached to the unit, which we all

attended. It was very small – just a couple of rooms – and there was little point in any of us being there. The teacher would try to coax us – 'Shall we try to do a little bit of learning?' – while we all ignored her. Most of the kids ran around, but I sat to one side, quiet and bored. Needless to say, I learned nothing. The only thing I liked about the school was that it had a gym. Sometimes, in the evenings, the staff would take us over to the gym and we'd play a game in which they'd turn off the lights and we'd hide. I enjoyed this because, being small and agile, I could find all sorts of hiding places, sometimes climbing to the top of the bars and lying on the topmost beam, just below the ceiling, where I could barely be spotted from below.

Although I hated the adolescent unit I liked most of the people there, staff and kids alike. Three people in particular stood out as special. There were two key workers, a couple called Paul and Alison, on the team who looked after us teenagers. I liked them because they treated us all like normal kids.

The other person I liked was Annie, the social worker attached to the unit. She was based in the school office there, and she was an outgoing, warm and cheerful woman who never asked me the sort of intrusive questions with which I was bombarded by most of the other staff members and the kids. She was always available, though. Annie clearly adored young people and knew how to relate to them. She didn't have to work out how to behave with me, she just knew. Soon I was gravitating to her office whenever I could. I would tell the teacher or nurse in charge that I wanted to talk to Annie, go over and knock on her door and then go in and sit on her lap. I had plucked up the courage to do this after I saw other kids do it. And when, the first time I tried it, Annie happily welcomed me onto her lap and cuddled me as if it was the most natural and normal thing in the world, I longed to go back for more. As with Mrs Gilbertson, I had found a rare person who showed me genuine affection and asked nothing in return. And for the frail, broken and unloved child that I was, it provided a small ray of warmth in an otherwise brutally bleak world.

I learned later that Annie and my social worker, Chris, knew each other well. Only years later did I discover that, in an attempt to understand more about my case, they had gone together to visit my father in prison. Annie told me that they had said to him, 'Gayle hasn't been able to tell us what happened the night her mother died. Can *you* tell us?' My father's unrepentant reply had been: 'Why don't I show you?' They had been shocked and I think after that they felt that there was no point at all in talking to him.

My father wrote to me regularly throughout my stay at Beech House. When his letters first began to arrive Annie asked me whether I wanted them. I told her that not only did I not want them, I didn't even want to know that they existed. She never mentioned them again, and I was grateful. But, although I knew she had to do it, I still hated the thought of her reading or even touching them.

From time to time I saw a psychiatrist in the unit, but we made little headway. He wanted me to talk about what had happened, but I couldn't, so mostly I sat in silence while he tried, and failed, to get me to open up. The staff in the unit also tried to get me to talk, believing that I might benefit. But what I felt none of them understood was that I needed to feel nurtured, cared for and protected if I was ever to feel safe enough to speak about what had happened. And I didn't feel any of these things: I felt extremely *un*safe and exposed. I was afraid not only that my father might walk in and claim me, but of most of the people around me.

My fears hadn't been helped by the aggressive behaviour of some of the older teenagers in the unit. They had tried to force me to join them in sniffing aerosols and when I'd refused they had held me down and forced me to. I didn't tell the staff what had happened, but after that I was constantly looking over my shoulder when any of them were around, afraid that it might happen again.

There were other incidents. One very disturbed boy went wild from time to time and on one occasion was restrained by the staff while they injected him in his bottom, presumably with a sedative. Another time he got hold of a knife and was threatening people with it, though the staff managed to remove it before he harmed himself or anyone else.

I did make a few friends, in particular a boy named Greg who was two years older than me. Just like me, Greg didn't understand why he was there. He was quieter than the others, and we sometimes talked or sat together. We became good friends and the staff said we looked like brother and sister. Greg made no demands on me and I made none on him. Neither of us ever asked the other why we were there. We didn't need to: we both knew that neither of us should have been there, and that was all there was to it. We often spent time together. In October 1987, when Britain was hit by the hurricane that weather forecaster Michael Fish had famously said was not on its way, Greg and I sat up all night, watching and listening to it, both of us terribly scared.

Apart from Greg, who I think felt the same way I did, only Annie seemed to understand that I was still in such a state of fear that until my basic need for safety was addressed no one would be able to reach me.

For several months after my arrival at Beech House I did little more than exist. I slept badly: my nightmares were almost constant. I ate very little and lost weight and, although I spoke to the staff and other kids when I needed to, I was totally unable to talk about my mother's death. I spent most of my time sitting alone and disconnected from those around me I and saw absolutely no one from my previous life. And my wish to die intensified to the point where I couldn't bear to be alive any longer. I knew that my father would soon be free, and what I feared, even more than the lonely hell I survived in, was that he would come for me.

I felt desperate to get away from the unit and I began to look for ways to escape. The doors and windows were always locked, but I was certain there had to be a way – and eventually I found it. In the kitchen there was a rubbish chute, used for all the kitchen waste, which led to a bin outside. This chute had a large opening – and I realised one day that it was big enough for me to get through. I waited for my chance and then slipped into the kitchen when no one was around. Sliding down the chute was absolutely disgusting. It was smeared with the filth of left-over food, peelings and refuse, but it was the only way out and the muck that smeared my clothes and hair was a small price to pay for a chance to escape. Once outside I headed across the grass towards the main road, but I was caught before I got to the front gate and marched back inside for a reprimand and a bath.

The next time I tried to escape it was with a girl named Lesley, who was a couple of years older than me and a lot more streetwise. We first spoke when she told me that she knew about my Mum. Her mother had attended the same church and had known my Mum, though not well, and when Mum died Lesley's mother had come home and talked about it. I didn't respond to this information – it was difficult to think of other people knowing about what had happened – but I liked Lesley and we became quite friendly.

One day Lesley said how much she'd like to get out and see her Mum. I said I would like to go too, so we hatched a plan together. A few days later we grabbed our chance and ran as fast as we could to the barbed-wire perimeter fence. We climbed over it, scratching ourselves in the process, and got into the field next to the hospital. We were sure they would look for us on the roads, so we decided to go cross-country.

We managed to cover the three miles from Chartham to Canterbury in a couple of hours and then to sneak onto a train – we had no money at all – to Folkestone. Once we'd crept off the train, unnoticed, we ran all the way to Louise's house. Louise's mother answered the door and although she must have known we weren't meant to be there she greeted me warmly and invited us in. To my delight Louise was home and she seemed happy to see me. Lesley and I stayed only five minutes, time enough for Louise to give me a present, a little brown and green Beanie Baby frog which I stuffed into my pocket.

Louise told me that she'd been upset when I'd disappeared, but she'd been told that I was going to a lovely place where I would be looked after and helped to get better. Her whole family believed this, she said. Years later, Louise would tell me that, had they known what would happen to me, her family would have offered me a home. But at the time they were told that I was being well cared for, and they had no idea how unhappy I was.

We didn't stay long. Lesley and I left again and headed to my old house. I wanted to see my brother, who was still living there with his girlfriend while the sale of the house went through. He wasn't in so we settled down to wait. We waited for him as long as we dared – several hours – and even tried to climb in through the window. I would have waited longer, but Lesley wanted to see her Mum, so we walked to her house, which was very close. By the time we arrived it was evening and we were hungry and exhausted. Her mother was surprised to see us, but was kind and gave us some food while she called the adolescent unit to let them know where we were.

A female member of staff arrived an hour or so later to collect us, in the unit's minibus. She was furious and was very unsympathetic. There was no 'Are you OK?', which might have been more appropriate in the circumstances. She made us sit apart in the bus and told us that we were in real trouble, so that by the time we got back I was feeling terrified.

The rest of the staff were also fairly angry with us, though they were not as enraged as the woman who'd been sent to fetch us was. We were told that as a punishment we would have to wear our pyjamas for a whole week and would not be allowed outside at all. This was bad enough, but what felt worse was that at first, no one ever said, 'You must have been very unhappy to run away', though a couple of days later Alison did say this. Her words made me feel a little better for a moment, but nothing really changed.

Awful as it was to have been sent back, I was glad I had seen Louise, even if only for a few minutes. I had been afraid that she'd forgotten me, or had stopped caring. The little toy frog she'd given me sat beside my bed, a reminder that I did still have a friend, even if I couldn't see her.

For the next few months, life continued much as before in the unit. I wondered how long I would have to stay and why I couldn't see anyone I knew. But no one would tell me anything. I did try to ask, but I wasn't managing to say a lot. And the answers I got were never clear. They'd say things like 'Maybe it would help if you had time away from everybody.' I knew it wouldn't: that was the last thing I needed, but I was confused and felt helpless and unable to change anything.

Then one day I was told that my grandparents would be allowed to visit me. The staff must have realised what they had tried so far wasn't helping and that I was desperately unhappy, so the rule banning visits to me was relaxed. My grandparents came, and so did Mrs Gilbertson. I was glad to see them, but the visits were awkward, especially with my grandparents. None of us could think of very much to say, and after half an hour they would say they had to be off, and I would watch them go, filled with a deep ache of longing and disappointment.

I thought about my old school friends all the time. I wondered whether they missed me at all, and whether they knew where I was. As Christmas approached I wrote cards to all of them. In each one I wrote 'Please don't forget me.' I begged the Beech House staff to let me take them to the school. But they refused to take me and did not offer to deliver the cards for me. Because I didn't have any addresses I had to throw the cards away, and with them any hope I had left that my friends might remember me or get in touch. I felt I had lost the last link I had with them and it was a bitter blow.

We had occasional outings from the unit – to go swimming, or for walks on the beach – and once a week we went to a local Safeway, where we were allowed to roam the store for half an hour to spend our pocket money. We were always taken out in the unit's white minibus, and I would try to get the seat next to the window so that I could stick my head out and feel the breeze on my face. That way it was easier not to think about anything, just to enjoy the feeling. Everyone in the surrounding area recognised the minibus and knew who we were. We'd see kids our own age shouting 'You're mental!' as we went past. There was nothing we could do but endure the humiliation.

The thought of dying was always in my mind, and eventually I decided to try to do something about it again. I blamed myself for my mother's death and believed that everyone else blamed me too. I felt I should have been able to prevent it and that I had been sent to prison because I couldn't. I felt so worthless that I believed I should be dead, that was all I was worthy of. Nothing would ever get better or change, I was sure of that, and oblivion seemed preferable.

I had managed to save some pocket money and on the next Safeway visit, unnoticed by the unit staff accompanying us, I went to the pharmacy and bought a tub of paracetamol, plus two more packets each containing fifty pills. I don't think a child would be able to buy that many pills today, but I wasn't questioned. I carried the pills back onto the bus in a paper bag, pretending I'd got sweets like everyone else.

Back at the unit I hid the paracetamol in my bunny pyjama case, which sat on my bed. I planned to take them one night, hoping that I would then fall asleep and die before I could be found in the morning. Two days later I put my plan into action. I waited until everyone had gone to bed and then began swallowing the paracetamol. It was hard getting so many pills down. They tasted disgusting and stuck in my throat. But I managed to take over sixty of them before I felt satisfied that I'd had enough and climbed into bed.

I lay waiting to fall asleep, but as the hours passed sleep would not come, and instead I felt more and more sick and very light-headed and dizzy. I wanted it to be quick, to fall asleep and never wake up, but that didn't happen. So I lay, for hour after hour, hearing my mother's words in my head, as she begged to me to get the police. The feelings I had when these flashbacks occurred were unbearable. Loss, grief, regret and, above all else, a certainty that I must be punished because I had failed to save her. At least when I was dead I could escape those awful feelings and thoughts.

But death was slow in coming. In the early hours of the morning I got out of bed and went to the duty nurse, who was sitting at the nursing station outside our bedrooms. I told her that I didn't feel well, and asked if I could have a bath. She said all right, and took me to run the tub. Then she left me there, telling me not to lock the door. I got into the bath feeling very ill. But I wanted to be clean when they found me. I managed to wash, and then got out of the bath. By this time I felt so faint, dizzy and sick that I couldn't stand any longer and had to sit down on the floor.

The nurse came in, and I told her I was OK and just needed to sit on the floor for a bit. You would imagine that a nurse in such a situation might ask questions, or insist on making checks, or at the very least help me. She did none of these things – she simply said, 'All right' and went away. I began to feel panicky and frightened. I didn't know what was happening in my body, which felt very strange, twitchy and out of control. I managed to get my pyjamas back on and get back to my bedroom, where I closed the door and collapsed on the floor.

The night nurse didn't check me again until morning,

when she found me, still slumped on the floor. I was semi-conscious, but I had no idea that I had been sick on the floor. A nurse tried to get me up onto my feet but I was limp and unable to stand. He said, 'Gayle, we've called an ambulance.' I whispered, 'I don't need an ambulance, I need a coffin.' Even in my half-comatose state I wanted only to be dead.

The paramedics who arrived minutes later got me into the ambulance and one of them sat beside me in the back and kept slapping my face, saying, 'Gayle, keep awake.' I felt the sting of the slaps, but I simply couldn't keep my eyes open.

When we got to hospital I was wheeled into a big room and laid on a bed with lots of equipment around me. Doctors were running about but all I could think was: 'When am I going to die? Am I nearly dead yet? Please let me die.'

My clothes were taken off and I lay on the bed in just my knickers, wishing that the nurses would cover me. I could hear a doctor saying: 'Gayle, you've taken a lot of pills, haven't you? You've done a lot of damage to yourself – I don't know if you are going to live.' Other doctors were talking to one another, saying my condition was very serious and mentioning liver damage.

As I drifted in and out of consciousness I became aware that my grandparents were standing near the bed, looking at me. Then I was being wheeled along, and I heard a voice say I was being taken to a ward. It was too late to pump my stomach, so they could only wait and see whether I was going to survive or not.

They decided not to take me to a children's ward because, in the circumstances, it wasn't deemed appropriate. Instead I was put in a ward full of women, most of whom had suffered miscarriages. 'What are you doing here?' one of them asked me when I came round. 'You're too young to have lost a baby.' I was confused. What *was* I doing here? As it sank in that I hadn't died and wasn't going to, I felt panicky and confused. Why hadn't all those pills worked? Was I really going to have to stay alive and face this awful existence?

I was in hospital for a week. During that time my grand-mother visited me several times. I remember her bringing me a nightdress from Marks and Spencer. Annie came too, and she brought me little easy-to-swallow jellies that she had made for me. Greg dropped by as well and left me his dressing gown and his watch, because I told him I had no way to tell what time it was. It turned out that – amazingly – my liver was not damaged. But my stomach was, and from then on would feel raw and sore most of the time. It has never fully recovered.

I was lucky to survive – but I didn't think so then, or for a long time afterwards. I lay in my hospital bed thinking that I should have died and wishing I had. I didn't know how I was going to face carrying on. I belonged nowhere, had no one and could see no prospect of a life with any joy or meaning in it. I wanted oblivion and an end to all my pain. But even that now seemed out of reach. Instead, once I was out of danger, I would be taken back to Beech House, to carry on with the bleak and lonely existence I had tried – and failed – to end.

II

Suicide watch

It was Annie who came to collect me from hospital and drive me back to Beech House. My stomach was still so sore that I couldn't stand upright properly and I walked slowly out to the car in a very fragile state. Annie was gentle and, as always, asked no intrusive questions. I was grateful for that. She took me into my room, where I climbed into bed and tried to sleep.

I didn't want to be back in the unit – or in my life. But it seemed that there was no escape from either. I could still barely take in the fact that, despite swallowing such a large number of pills, I had survived. I didn't want to be alive. I wanted to be dead and I felt distraught that I hadn't managed even that.

I was considered to be still suicidal and was put on twenty-four-hour watch, which meant that I was never able to be alone. For the next couple of weeks a member of staff accompanied me everywhere I went, keeping an eye on me as I sat in the day room, waiting outside the loo door for me, and even watching me all night as I slept. My bedroom was such a tiny box of a place that they could barely fit inside it, so they left the door open and sat on a chair just outside. Being watched like this felt like the ultimate invasion of my privacy, and because I was a very private person it was almost unbearable.

The weekend after I came out of hospital I was allowed to go and stay with my grandparents, which gave me some respite. They had obviously been warned that I had to be watched, and when I arrived my grandmother told me that she had put all tablets and medication out of reach so that I wouldn't be tempted. I was pleased to get away from Beech House, even though it was only for a short time, but neither I nor my grandparents were relaxed about the visit and I felt more than ever that I didn't belong anywhere or with anyone.

When I returned to Beech House I was told that I would be allowed to go back to my grandparents for forty-eight hours over Christmas. Again, this had to be better than staying at the unit but I was acutely aware that my grandparents were doing what they felt they must, rather than actually wanting me.

Three days before Christmas, on 22 December, Annie came to see me and told me gently that my father was to be released on 4 January. Although she didn't comment on the sentence, I'm sure she wasn't any happier about it than I was. He had spent just under fourteen months in custody. All I could think was: 'He's free – while I am still in prison.'

It seemed to me that I had been given a longer sentence than he had. It horrified me to think that he was out and could find me once again. I was so afraid that he would talk the authorities into letting him have me back.

I didn't feel able to tell Annie of my fears, but she knew enough about me to understand how I would feel. She promised that my father would never be allowed to have me back, and that he wouldn't even be allowed to contact me. But I couldn't see how this could be enforced. I remained terrified and the idea that he would soon be free dominated my thoughts.

And, as later events would prove, I was right to be frightened. It would take more than a few authorities to prevent him from contacting me. The social-services records of the time confirm that they knew I was scared and give an insight into officialdom's growing understanding of the threat that my father presented. I had never told anyone how I felt, but Annie and Chris would have picked up on it from my behaviour. The only thing I had ever said directly was after the prison visit to my father, when I had told Chris and Dr Hayter that I never wanted to see him again. I had also refused to read his letters to me and I'm sure they could see how terrified I was every time he was even mentioned.

In fact, as I learned much later when I read my files, social services took out an injunction against him when he came out of prison, forbidding him to contact me directly. He could only go through them to have news of me. I wasn't told of this at the time – perhaps I was considered to be too young – but Annie's reassurance that he wouldn't be allowed to contact me obviously referred to it. However, even if I had known of this legal move, I wouldn't have felt safer. I knew that my father had never respected the law and would have enjoyed looking for ways to flout it.

In the minutes of a social-services meeting at this time, at which Chris, Annie and others were present, it was said that 'Gayle has great fears about Dad sneaking up on her.' It continued: 'It was considered that Mr Sanders is a powerful man and the sentence hasn't really touched him. When things aren't going his way he can be dangerous. It is felt that he cannot see Gayle's needs and feelings . . . concerns were expressed about his ability to manipulate and persuade people to his opinion, to have people take pity on him, particularly it seems from men. It was considered that if he is crossed he may well turn his wrath upon the statutory agencies.' The report also said that while in an open prison my father had gone out and about quite easily, not even with the prison wardens but with members of the clergy.

Another report from the same period made it clear that my father had believed that during the custody case there had been a conspiracy between the judge and the Court Welfare Officer to deprive him of guardianship of me. It said that he had tried to pursue this complaint, even to Home Office level, but that Michael Howard, who had then been Home Secretary, had refused to take it on. It

also said that the parole officer speculated 'as to what Mr
Sanders will do when he finds himself completely blocked,
taking into consideration what happened when he was
refused Gayle's custody.'

My terror of my father was clearly justified. A growing
number of people had realised that he might do anything
to get what he wanted. And he still wanted me. I wasn't
convinced that anyone could protect me from him, and as
his release date approached I barely slept or ate.

However, the date came and went and I heard nothing
more. I heard that soon after he had left prison he had
gone back to live with his mother and was studying
theology, with the intention of becoming ordained as a
priest. Far from diminishing my fears, this only confirmed
that not only was my father living in the area again but
that he was as cunning and devious as ever. He was simply
developing a new 'acceptable' social image which would
win him friends and supporters.

Early in the New Year of 1988 I was told that I would be
going back to my old school twice a week. The idea, I was
told, was to prepare me for moving on, hopefully to a foster
home. I had already been at Beech House far longer than
most of the other teenagers there. The majority stayed six
months at most – my friend Greg had left along with all
the others whom I had known in the beginning. But the
authorities couldn't leave me there for ever, especially as I
was so unhappy. Even though no foster home had yet been

found for me, the doctors obviously felt it was time to rein-
troduce me to the outside world. I was already getting used
to being brought up without a family or anyone in particular who would care for me or think I was special. There
was clearly a danger that I would become totally institu-
tionalised.

While I was glad to see my old friends, especially Louise,
the twice-weekly visits – intended to allow me to adapt
slowly – were not such a good idea. I felt that by attending
school only two days a week I was drawing attention to
myself and was neither fully there nor fully absent. It was
an uncomfortable halfway house which meant that I
couldn't follow the threads of school life, either in studies
or in friendships, because of everything that happened on
the days when I wasn't there. And I couldn't stay late after
school for any sporting or other activities because my
journey to school and back again each time took two hours.
I had to leave at six-thirty each morning and was dropped
at Canterbury bus station in the minibus. From there I had
to get two buses, first to Folkestone and from there to
Hythe. In the evening I did the whole thing in reverse,
getting back to Beech House at around six in the evening.
I hated the travel, which I found exhausting. And I felt
confused about the purpose of sending me to school twice
a week. I didn't understand what the point was. But then,
I saw no point to my life anyway, and it seemed to me that
this was just another meaningless exercise.

After a few weeks of this arrangement it became clear

to me that the authorities in charge of my case didn't know what to do with me. They had searched for a foster home without success and there didn't appear to be anywhere they could send me. Once again I felt utterly unwanted and desperate. Every other child in the world, it seemed to me, had a home to go to and someone who wanted them. But not me. I went through the motions of my life at school and at Beech House, so unhappy that I wished many times I had managed to kill myself.

After the social services files of available foster parents had been exhausted, Chris told me they wanted to advertise for a foster family for me. Reluctantly, I agreed – I felt terribly exposed, but it would be worth it if I found a family. The ad was put in the local newspaper – a typical 'Would you like to foster this child?' ad. It listed my interests and needs – Gayle loves sport and would like a secure home with a loving family, and so on – but there were no replies. This left me feeling utterly unwanted. Not only did everyone who knew me not want me, but even a stranger wouldn't offer to take me.

Next I was taken on visits to a couple of children's homes, but I hated them. They seemed to me to be little better than Beech House and I was relieved when I was told that I wouldn't have to go to any of them if I didn't want to.

I began to wonder if I was ever going to leave Beech House but then I was told that social services had at last found a potential foster family. A teacher at my school, Mrs Davis, had offered to have me. I knew her, but not well, and I liked her and thought she was very pretty. I was also aware that she knew my father, but I was so desperate to leave the unit that I said nothing about this and agreed to go on a weekend visit to her home. Lesley and her husband Mark had never fostered before, but had come forward after hearing about me, presumably through the school, and were willing to give me a temporary home. They had a young daughter, Millie, and the family lived in Folkestone, not far from the school. It was a kind gesture by a teacher who clearly cared very much that one of the school's pupils was without a home and wanted to do her best to help.

I was dropped off at their house one Friday evening for a trial visit. After a pleasant welcome I was shown to my room before we sat down to dinner. I was extremely nervous and anxious, uncertain about whether they would want me or I would like them, so I was able to eat very little and soon went up to bed.

The next morning I was lying in bed when Mark walked into my room, without knocking, a glass of orange juice in his hand. He said good morning and put the glass down on the bedside table. Then he sat on my bed and started chatting. His proximity and familiarity made me very nervous and I turned over with my face to the wall and my back towards him to show him that I didn't feel comfortable and he should leave. At that point he started rubbing my shoulders and back and I froze, alarm bells screeching in my head. I kept asking myself 'Am I overreacting? Is he just trying to be friendly? Perhaps I just don't know how to accept someone being kind.' But while my head tried to reason, my body had no doubts. This was a potentially threatening situation and I could barely breathe, let alone move.

Eventually Mark went away, leaving me in a state of terror. What on earth was I going to do? In retrospect I was obviously unable to recognise a caring gesture, but at the time I thought that I couldn't possibly stay there. If his actions hadn't been innocent then what might happen the next night? I got up and went down to breakfast, where I asked Lesley if she could possibly take me back to Beech House to get my favourite T-shirt. 'OK – Mark will take you, won't you, Mark?' she said. Again I froze, but I had no choice. After breakfast we got into the car and I sat, rigid and silent, as Mark drove me to Beech House.

Once I got inside I flew to my room, where I crawled under the bed. The staff soon discovered where I was and tried to coax me out while Mark waited outside for me. But I wasn't going to move. I stayed under the bed for several hours, long after Mark had given up and left. They kept asking me what had happened but I couldn't speak – the events of that morning had sent me back into a traumatised state. But when I finally emerged later that afternoon they understood enough not to suggest sending me back to the Davises' house again.

I never did tell anyone what had happened. In hindsight, I'm sure Mark meant well and had been doing his best to

sympathise with me and would no doubt have been horrified to realise how badly his actions had affected me. But
I was a frightened child and I couldn't even explain the
problem, let alone try again.

We were back to square one and the authorities were
wringing their hands in frustration at what to do with me.
Then, a couple of weeks later, I was told that my grandparents had agreed that I could stay with them temporarily
while the search for a foster home continued. The circumstances were never discussed but I imagined that social
services must have approached them and explained that
they had nowhere else to place me and simply couldn't
keep me at Beech House any longer.

I may have been wrong but at the time I felt certain that
Gran and Grandad were accepting me out of guilt. I
couldn't help but feel that if they had really wanted me
they would have asked me to come and live with them
immediately after my mother died. I reasoned that if they
hadn't wanted me before, then they probably didn't really
want me now. I knew they would have been put under pressure to take me, and I didn't want to be there on such
terms. However, I had no choice, and being with them was
certainly better than being at Beech House.

I went to stay with my grandparents in May 1988, after
eleven months at the adolescent unit. I felt very uncomfortable with the situation and suspected they did, too. I
loved them, but I also felt confused and let down by them,
and I was acutely aware that this arrangement was tempo-

rary and that I would soon be moved somewhere else. It meant that I couldn't relax or settle in – and this feeling was reinforced by the fact that they put me in the guest room and referred to it as such, rather than suggesting that I might call it *my* room.

I was also very worried that my father might hear where I was. I knew that he had been told I was living with my maternal grandparents and I was sure that he would come and 'get' me or them. He was living at his mother's house, not far away, and I didn't want my grandparents to be put in the awful position of having to deal with him. I felt I was putting them in an unpredictable situation – this was the one thing that made me glad the arrangement was only temporary.

The months that I spent with my grandparents were very mixed. They were kind to me, but remained fairly distant. When I was small my grandparents had been one of my few sources of cuddles and physical affection and I had idolised them and looked forward eagerly to seeing them every time we visited. But too much had happened and something had changed irrevocably. None of us had recovered from my mother's death, and I could not forget – or get over – their abandonment of me afterwards. Those weeks I had spent with Louise's family, waiting for my own to come for me, were constantly on my mind and the hurt of that rejection was still horribly raw.

Nothing could take away the sense that nobody wanted me. My grandparents hadn't wanted me then and I was uncertain that they wanted me now. I felt they had probably only taken me in because no one else would. Mostly they didn't speak of my mother, or about what had happened; they simply got on with the practicalities of life. But I did ask Gran if she had a photograph of my mother that I could have. She looked through her photographs and gave me two. One of them was my mother on her wedding day – with my father beside her. The other was a picture of my mother, father, brother, sister and I, all together, when I was a baby.

I found it very hard to see my mother beside the man who had killed her. And the woman in those photos wasn't the Mum I remembered: it was a woman I didn't know, at a time when she had been much younger. However, Gran told me there were no recent photos of my mother. So I took the ones she gave me, cut my father out of the wedding photo, and have kept that small, battered picture of my mother with me from that time on.

I still had not grieved for my mother. Life since her death had simply been a continuation of the trauma, and all my feelings of grief and loss were deeply buried. But that small photo gave me a connection to her that, even in my numbed state, meant a great deal.

12

Lost in trauma

On the surface my grandparents and I tried to behave as normally as possible. On Saturdays I went shopping with Gran and I remember helping with the shopping bags and sometimes holding her hand. That was the only physical contact we had. I would get a video to watch for the afternoon and we'd get custard tarts because Gran liked them. My grandfather liked watching *Spitting Image* and the *Carry On* films and I would sometimes watch with him, or play Scrabble with Gran. And there were a handful of visits from other members of the family – I remember my Uncle David and his family coming over. And a few times I saw my brother and sister.

Though we went through the motions of a normal life, there was no permanence in my world any more. I didn't know whether Gran and Grandad wanted me there, I didn't know whether they liked having me around and I didn't know how long I would be able to stay. I lived on a knife-edge of uncertainty and I never felt that

I could afford to let myself relax or get comfortable.

While I was with them I began having nightmares in which I saw my mother in the room, a shadowy, haunted figure, and heard my father breaking into the house. There had been many previous nightmares in the past three years, most of them about my mother's death, but these seemed to carry on when I woke, so that I no longer knew what was real and what wasn't. The images of my Mum were so vivid in the night that I really believed she was there. Sadly, there was no comfort in seeing her, because I was so frightened.

Unable to stay in my room alone, I would go into my grandparents' room and, fearful of waking them, stand at the bottom of their bed until my grandmother woke. Then I would tell her that I had heard noises and someone was trying to get in. I never said that I saw my mother. Gran was not unkind; she would tell me to go back to bed, and sometimes, when I was very distressed, she would let me get in beside her.

Without doubt I was very disturbed. I had already been through so much, and living with my grandparents had brought me much closer to the realisation that my mother really had gone. So many feelings of loss and grief were buried inside me, and since I couldn't express them they surfaced through the nightmares.

I was now back at my old school full-time and, while it wasn't easy to settle back in after such a long gap, I was glad that at least I was going in every day, like the others, and so wasn't drawing attention to myself any longer. Mrs Davis had left the school, and I was relieved that I wouldn't have to see her. And while Mrs Gilbertson was still there, I seldom saw her because she was teaching in the lower school and I was now in the upper school. It was around this time that I joined the local trampoline club. I had tried it at school and had always liked it, and I wanted to do more.

The coach at the club was called Mike, a down-to-earth man who always ate Granny Smith apples as he coached us. I liked the fact that all he was interested in was my ability on the trampoline and not my circumstances. He was an excellent coach and I enjoyed training with him.

I began training at the trampoline club two or three evenings a week, and found I was good at it. I soon began entering competitions and went on to win a number of awards and to compete at national level. When so much else in my life was chaotic, my love of trampolining gave me a focus that meant a lot to me.

My grandparents still lived in Dover, so I had a one-and-a-half-hour bus journey to school each day, which meant I got home at half past five – later if I went to the after-school club which I did most of the time. When I got home my grandmother would have dinner ready – she was an excellent cook and for the first time in my life I was given delicious, nourishing food at predictable times each day. However, after spending so long on an irregular diet and avoiding the ghastly food at Beech House, it was a struggle to make myself eat properly. I loved it that Gran was a good cook but, no matter how enticing the meals she prepared, I could only get a small part of them down.

I was very thin: at fourteen I weighed the same as I had at twelve and still hadn't started my periods. But now I began to worry that I was fat. This idea grew stronger and stronger in my mind, so I would sit at my grandparents' table and toy with the food, eating little or nothing. Grandad would always say 'You eat like a bird' and 'You need fattening up' but Gran would tell him to leave me alone. She never pushed any food on me, which I was grateful for. Perhaps she realised that I was on the verge of an eating disorder, and perhaps she also sensed that pushing someone who is in such a delicate state can only make things worse.

At the time I was convinced that I was just making sure I didn't get fat. Looking back, it's clear that I was under-eating quite dramatically. I ate no breakfast, seldom had any lunch and only nibbled at my dinner. I think there were a number of reasons for this. Firstly, it was the one thing in my painfully difficult life that I could control. It was also true that I didn't want to get bigger and develop curves like the other girls of my age. I didn't want to grow up, feeling that there was nothing to grow up *for*. I was still just existing from day to day, and continued to feel that it would be easier to die than to live.

But there was another aspect to this attempt to keep myself physically immature. I still wanted to be a little girl because deep down I believed that if only I could go back and be a child again I could be a good kid and make things better and rewrite history. If I could do that I could save my mother. I wanted to be able to turn the clock back and create a different outcome.

Of course, while desperately wishing that this were possible, I knew that it wasn't, and so undereating was also a way of punishing myself – through deprivation. I still felt terrible, constant guilt. I believed that I should have been able to do something to prevent my mother's death, and that I deserved to be punished because I hadn't.

I was suffering from anorexia, although that wasn't the way I thought of it at the time, but I continued to undereat, and to have difficulty eating, for many years. Given this, perhaps it seems surprising that I was able to be so sporty, playing every game available at school and achieving real success in my trampolining and later in dance too. I can only say that the human body is astonishing: I'm not sure myself how I managed it, but I did somehow find the stamina and energy I needed to be very physically active, despite my frugal diet.

Perhaps it worked the other way around too. Maybe the importance of sport in my life and the resultant need to eat so as to maintain my energy levels was what stopped me from starving myself even more. In fact, I think that sport was also one of the things that stopped me from turning to drink or drugs. When I was playing netball, hockey, rounders, trampolining or dancing, I stopped thinking and worrying. For that brief time I wasn't anxious or suicidal, I was just immersed in what I was doing. I loved that feeling, which was why I spent as much time as I could on sports.

Once I was back at the school I was able to resume my friendship with Louise. We were no longer as close as we had once been, because we were now in different friendship groups. While Louise had joined one crowd of girls, I became friends with a girl called Suzie and a couple of others, Charlotte and Eleanor. But although Louise and I were to some extent going our separate ways, our friendship remained. Both of us were very loyal and we looked out for one another. My friendship with her was one of the very few reminders of the life I'd had before Mum's death, and it meant a great deal to me.

Although I was still very quiet and found it hard to talk to most adults, I was able to relate much better to friends of my own age, and this was very important to me. I didn't confide in these friends about my deepest feelings and thoughts, but I did join in games and activities and enjoy being with them and this gave my life a much-needed element of normality. I didn't, of course, have much in common with my peer group. But I made a huge effort to be part of things because it always felt terribly important to me to have friends. Nonetheless, while the other girls were becoming interested in boys, clothes and make-up, I didn't think about these things at all. My life was about survival and nothing more.

While I was at my grandparents' place the hunt went on for a home for me. Another ad was placed in the local paper, and once again there were no replies and I felt humiliated. People could get rid of most things through the small ads, I thought, but a child seemed to be of no interest.

Eventually Chris asked me what I would think about going to a boarding school. By this time I had been at my grandparents' house for several months and Chris said that they had agreed that if I went to a boarding establishment then they would have me for the holidays. I understood that for them a holidays-only arrangement would feel more manageable, but I hated the idea of leaving my day school and going somewhere new. Although things had never been quite the same for me after the time I had missed while I was at Beech House, it was at least familiar for me and I had friends there. So I told Chris I really didn't want to go. But as it became clear that no other alternative had been found, I began to see that I might after all have to change schools and board.

I absolutely dreaded leaving, and hoped desperately that it wouldn't have to happen. I couldn't bear the idea of starting all over again – it would feel like another prison, as bad as the adolescent unit. I had already lost everyone when I was sent there. Was it about to happen again?

Resigned to what seemed the inevitable, I told my friends and my favourite teachers at school that I would soon be going. Louise and my other friends promised to keep in touch. And the teachers said they were sorry to see me go too.

A few days later, Chris came to see me and said that one of the teachers at school, a PE teacher called Mrs Minter had offered to foster me. I knew her well and liked her. She was a small, sporty woman with lots of energy and enthusiasm. But I was very surprised that she had offered to take me. I couldn't understand why she would want me. Perhaps she had realised how upset I was about having to go to boarding school.

It was astonishing that a second teacher from my school had now offered to foster me. But this very fact also made me nervous. Mrs Davis had offered to foster me and it had been a disaster which lasted only one night. Would it work out any better with Mrs Minter? Offering to take me into her family was enormously kind of her and I appreciated her generosity. But to take me into her home, to join her family, was a big step.

I was pleased, but confused too. I couldn't believe that anyone wanted me or liked me, but I was very glad I would be able to stay at the school. But there was a nagging worry in my mind too. I had suspected that Mrs Davis had known my father. Did Mrs Minter know him too? I had no idea, but the thought that she might worried me. But, uneasy as I was about it, I preferred to risk being with someone who might know my father rather than being sent to boarding school, away from everyone and everything I knew.

It was November when the Minters came forward – six

months after I had gone to live with my grandparents. For the next three months I went on regular weekly visits to their home, until in the spring of 1989, soon after I turned fifteen, I moved in with them.

Shortly before I left my grandparents it was Valentine's Day. I was very keen that my grandparents should buy one another a card and a little gift. I encouraged each of them, separately, to do so and I was very pleased when they did. I suspect they did it to humour me, and thought it was a lot of fuss about nothing. But somehow it meant a lot to me that they should show they loved one another.

Leaving their home after nine months was hard, and I think we all felt sad and didn't know what to say. I was resigned to having to go, but in my heart I wished desperately that they would stop me at the door and say, 'Wait, Gayle, please stay, we do love you.' But they didn't say a word, or even acknowledge that I was leaving. I left for school as usual on a Thursday morning; Chris came to pick me up straight from class and take me to my new foster parents.

13

Clinging on

Julie Minter and her husband Paul lived in Folkestone and had two adorable children, Dominic and Daisy, aged four and six. Julie was small, with short brown hair, and Paul was of average height with a round belly and not much hair.

Theirs was a busy household, with both parents working and two very lively kids. I found the children very easy to be with and was very happy to help look after them or to babysit. I used to do Daisy's hair for her, read to them, play with them and make up lots of games. They were too young to resent my presence and they accepted me in the way that very young children do, easily and affectionately, as another playmate. For me, after so much rejection, this unquestioning acceptance was wonderful, and I loved being with them.

My relationship with their parents was a little more complicated. Julie and Paul were nice people. He was the headmaster of another local school and they were both friendly and kind to me. But from the beginning I felt their ideas about life with me were a little optimistic. I think they believed that once I was in a nice family and a nice home, I would be able to settle down and get on with life. They had little idea of quite how big an impact the trauma I had suffered had made on me and I was unable to tell them. As a result, I felt constantly under pressure to meet their expectations.

Trying to fit into someone else's home, however nice they are, is difficult under the best of circumstances. For me, after the loss of my mother and two and a half years of feeling unwanted, unloved and a headache to everyone, trying to become part of a new family was daunting, frightening and bewildering. No doubt it was very hard for them too. They had bravely taken on a teenager who couldn't have been in a worse state emotionally, and they were trying to help. But, sadly, all too often their efforts simply made me more anxious than ever.

Unable to manage a lot of contact, I spent hours in my bedroom. But Paul, no doubt meaning well, would knock on the door and say, 'I don't understand you, Gayle – why are you up in your bedroom? Come downstairs with us.' Reluctantly I would go downstairs, only to feel awkward, in the way, unable to think of anything to say and desperate to run back upstairs again.

I was grateful that they had taken me in, but I found it almost impossible to behave in the way they seemed to assume I should be able to. I came to dread the note of accusation in Paul's voice when he asked me, yet again, why I wanted to be in my room and not with them. He simply had no idea how hard it was for me, and I couldn't tell him.

I couldn't sit at table and eat a normal meal, or chat about my day. I couldn't relax with the Minters and watch television, or have friendly discussions. I still found it terribly difficult to speak any more than I absolutely had to, I still hunched my shoulders over as though I was trying to shrink out of sight, and I still felt barely able to get through from one day to the next. Mealtimes were particularly difficult, because Julie, concerned about my weight, chided me constantly about not eating enough. The trouble was, I simply couldn't manage to get food down and I sat miserably at the table until I was finally allowed to go.

Try as I might to fit in – and I did try, by helping as much as I could with the children – my feeling of being unwanted was undiminished. I liked Julie and Paul, I loved their kids and I thought their home was beautiful. But I wasn't really part of any of it: they weren't my family, they were just letting me live with them. I was still simply existing, and still wishing, as I closed my eyes each night, that I wouldn't ever have to wake up again.

The Minters made an effort to be pleasant to me, but I was very aware that they didn't treat me the way they treated their own children. How could they? I wasn't their child, I was the troubled teenager they had taken on and no doubt they often felt frustrated by my silence and withdrawal. Inevitably they would do things as a family and even though I might have chosen to stay at home, although I'd been invited to join them, I still felt so left out.

I was also still terrified that my father might appear. And it seems that the authorities were concerned too. Though nothing was said to me, a social-services report written just before I moved in with the Minters stated that: 'The Panel may wish to consider the provision of a security system for Mr and Mrs Minter's house. It is unlikely that Mr Sanders would attempt to approach Gayle or the family but the potential is there and those involved with him believe he is a dangerous man.' No security system was installed and I don't know whether the Minters were ever actually warned about my father because Julie and Paul never indicated to me in any way that they were aware of, or worried about, my father.

In fact, an incident that happened some months after my arrival seemed to confirm that, far from being wary of my father, they were, as I had feared, actually friendly with him.

At this stage, although things were far from perfect at the Minters', I was managing. Then one day the phone rang and I picked it up. The voice on the other end asked for Julie. I recognised it immediately and dropped the phone. It was my father.

Julie then picked up the phone and, in front of me, had a chatty conversation with him. I stood staring at her throughout, unable to believe that she was talking amiably to my father, even if she didn't know how afraid of him I was.

At the end of the call Julie put down the phone, turned to me and said, 'He sounded very chirpy.' Then she went off into the kitchen to cook dinner. I was horrified. I felt totally betrayed and very, very unsafe. I realised that Julie was not going to understand or protect me. Her tone with my father was genuinely friendly. She was yet another person he had beguiled with his charming, easy manner. I was shocked and confused. I felt that she should have said to him, 'This is not appropriate.' Then she should have asked me how I felt about it and phoned my social worker, Chris, to let her know what had happened. Instead she had not only behaved as though my father calling was perfectly normal and acceptable, but she seemed unaware of my distress.

Part of me realised that Julie must have no comprehension of how I felt. I knew she must have been given the facts about my mother's death and what had happened to me since. But she clearly had no idea how terrified of my father I still was.

I never recovered from the effects of that phone call and Julie's response to it. Although I was to remain with the Minters for a year and a half, after that episode I withdrew even deeper into myself, convinced I could never trust either Julie or Paul and feeling more isolated and alone than ever. I also felt desperately unsafe, knowing that Julie would not protect me from my father.

With hindsight, I think that Julie and Paul were well-intentioned people who were out of their depth in trying to take on a traumatised, despairing teenager who had a multitude of problems. I probably seemed to them like a silent, sullen adolescent who needed bringing out of herself. But I couldn't just snap out of the state I was in – I needed endless amounts of patience, security and acceptance before I could even begin that process and quite possibly only a couple with specialised training could have helped me.

I think Julie and Paul felt that firm boundaries and a family environment would be enough. Unfortunately it wasn't that simple. I needed acceptance, warmth and love. And most of all I needed to feel safe. But once again, because of the proximity of my father, that was the very last thing I felt.

This wasn't helped by my visits to my Nan's where he was living. It may seem extraordinary that I went round to her house at that time, but I was desperate to maintain the few family relationships I had. At this stage I very rarely saw my brother and sister, or any other relatives, and I didn't want to lose Nan too. Of course I was also very anxious not to be anywhere near my father. So Chris arranged for me to visit Nan once a fortnight, during which time my father was to be out of the house. These visits continued for some time. But although my father wasn't there, seeing his things and knowing he was living there made me feel sick. It would have been much better for us to meet elsewhere, but no one ever suggested it.

Nan and I would go through the pretence of normality, but it was impossible to maintain. I was tense, nervous and jumpy, terrified that my father might be there after all, or might return. And Nan didn't help. Far from recognising my fears, she would try to get me to read letters that he had left for me, no doubt hoping that all the pieces could somehow be put back together and we would be a family once more. She had never fully accepted what my father had done and had obviously forgiven him, as had my brother and sister, who were still in regular contact with him. She probably found it hard to understand that I didn't feel the same way.

Sometimes I read his letters, because I didn't know how to say no to Nan's urgings. They were bland, full of chat about nothing, but I still hated them, and hated having to read them. Nan tried to get me to write to him and would say things to me like, 'You will get him a birthday card, won't you?' and I felt I had to, although it was the last thing I wanted to do.

One day a few weeks later, as I was walking home from school, I turned to see him in his car, following me. He drew up beside me and stopped. So shocked and frightened that I could barely breathe, I turned and ran towards the house, where I raced inside and slammed the door.

It happened again, a few weeks later. This time my father drove up and down the road, passing me each time, as I walked home. He didn't stop, and once again I ran home in a state of panic. Once inside the house I ran up to my room and curled up on the bed, my heart pounding, my body shaking. I felt absolute horror.

I didn't tell anyone, not even Chris. I didn't think there was any point because I believed that no one could stop him doing as he pleased. But after that I was never able to leave the house without fearing that I might see him again. The nightmares and flashbacks that had always haunted me became worse, as did my anxiety. He knew exactly where I was, and could watch me or follow me at any time. Just as I had feared. I was still not free of him and was afraid that I never would be.

During this time I was once again seeing Dr Hayter. My visits to her were now on a regular basis, but although I still liked her and appreciated her genuine concern for me, we continued to spend in complete silence most of the fifty minutes that each session lasted. I was no nearer to being able to talk about my feelings than I had been when I first saw her soon after my mother's death.

At a loss over what to do with me, Dr Hayter and Chris took me to the Royal Free Hospital in Hampstead, London, to see Dr Dora Black, the only psychiatrist in the country specialising in the psychological impact on children of the killing of one parent by the other. She had written a book called *When Father Kills Mother*. I hadn't read it, and I knew nothing about her, but I agreed to go and meet her. I knew immediately that she was someone – the first person I had ever met – who had genuine insight into how I was feeling. The things she said were so accurate, things that no one had ever said to me before. I didn't have to explain anything to her: she knew.

In a very calm, almost matter-of-fact way, Dr Black said to me, 'I guess you feel you have lost everything, don't you? You lost your home and your family as well as your mother, didn't you? And I imagine you haven't been able to grieve for your mother. I expect you must have a lot of nightmares and flashbacks.'

I stared at her, almost unable to believe that at long last someone knew what was going on. Until then I felt I had always been treated like a bereaved child who had lost a parent. But most children in that situation still have the other parent, or at least some family. I had lost absolutely everything, and now, for the first time, this was being acknowledged. Dora Black wasn't surprised that I hadn't talked – she knew why it had been impossible. And not only did she know so much but she said it in such a comfortable, easy way. She was familiar and at ease with a subject which made most people nervous and awkward.

Dora Black recommended to Dr Hayter and Chris that I should be placed with specialist therapeutic foster carers and have therapy three or four times a week.

Dr Hayter must have been struck by Dora Black's insights too, because as we came out of the room she put her arm around me. Startled, I shrugged it off. Adults had rarely hugged or cuddled me at that time; I wasn't used to being touched by anyone but Julie and Paul's children. But I was sorry that I had given her the impression I didn't like it, and I wished I had let her hug me because it was what I wanted and needed. But I never forgot that gesture, or that she was trying to reach out to me and offer warmth.

As for Dora Black's recommendations, no doubt they would have helped me a great deal – had they been carried out. But there was no specialist foster carer available. And presumably no one was able to pay for, or take me to, several sessions a week with Dora or any other therapist. So my life went on very much as it had before.

At school I was studying for my GCSEs, which I was due to take the following summer. At that stage I cared very little about school work, not because I didn't have a sense of the value of education – I always did – but because of the state I was in. I found it difficult to concentrate and made only as much effort as I had to in order to remain average. I had missed a large chunk of my studies while I was in Beech House – where I learned nothing – and that didn't help. The French teacher at school decided I had missed so much that I couldn't rejoin the class and made me spend French lessons sitting alone in an area reserved for pupils who had misbehaved. Every time I sat there teachers passing by would stop to ask 'What have you done?' and although I was able to reply 'Nothing' I hated being there and being isolated from the rest of the class.

While school work was tough, I still enjoyed all kinds of sports, and still went twice a week to the trampoline club. I also took up modern dance, training in the subject at a local dance school run by a very nice woman called Leila, who had taught an after-school dance club at my school. She was a popular and talented teacher and I got on with her very well. I loved dancing in the same way that I loved all my sports: while I was being physically active, I wasn't thinking about anything other than what I was doing. It released me from the endless anxious thoughts that whirled around my brain.

Soon after moving in with the Minters I had made friends with a girl at school called Suzie, who lived very close to their home. While I was still good friends with Louise, her house was now some distance away and I began travelling to and from school with Suzie and spending time at her place. Suzie lived with her parents and her elder brother and I liked them all. Her Mum always made sure that the house was immaculate, while her Dad was a very energetic man. The whole family made me feel welcome and were always friendly and accommodating to me.

During the winter, when Suzie and I were both sixteen, it snowed a lot and Suzie, her Dad and I went tobogganing. We had a lot of fun in the snow and on the way back her Dad pulled us both on the toboggan so that we could sit down all the way home. I thought it was very sweet of him. I often stayed the night at Suzie's – it made a welcome break from the Minters.

I also made friends, around this time, with a boy at the school. His name was Dan. He asked me if I wanted to go to Chessington World of Adventures one day, and I said yes. But even though it wasn't really a date, I was so nervous that I got Suzie and her boyfriend to come too.

Dan and I got on really well and we went out together a few times. A relationship might have developed, but I just wasn't ready for one, and he seemed happy simply for us to get to know one another. We became close friends and I recognised him as someone very loyal and trustworthy. He always treated me with respect and concern and I knew I could rely on him. Our friendship went a long way towards helping me to develop trust in a man.

Despite friendships like Suzie's and Dan's, which meant a great deal to me, I was still deeply unhappy. I did put on a little weight, and my periods started, though very sporadically. And I did go to school and do my best to study. But the year after arriving at the Minters' I did poorly in my GCSEs, passing only a small handful with low grades. I felt useless and embarrassed but at the same time I couldn't see any point in passing exams when I didn't even want to live. Exams were for people with prospects. They simply didn't fit into my bleak and meaningless view of things. I didn't think about the future because I didn't want a future, and I didn't want one because I couldn't see one.

The school wasn't brilliant, academically, so although some of my friends had passed their GCSEs and were leaving school, or moving into the sixth form, others were staying on to do retakes. I had to decide what to do, and I chose to stay at the school and take my GCSEs again the following summer. Not because I had changed the way I felt or seen a bright tomorrow for myself, but because I didn't know what else to do. School seemed preferable to leaving and trying to find a job when I had no qualifications, and my friends Louise and Suzie were doing retakes too, so I thought that at least we would be together.

I limped on through the next school year, managing to make myself study so that I wouldn't fail again. Despite my unhappiness and lack of direction, there was now a part of me that knew I wanted to pass my exams and also knew that I needed to concentrate if I was to make any kind of future for myself.

14

Despair

In the spring half-term break, just before I turned seventeen, I went on a skiing holiday in France with the
Minters. Julie's sister Stacey and brother-in-law Josh
came with us. I had never met them before – they lived
some distance away from us and on the occasions when
Julie and Paul had gone to visit them I had not gone
along. This was often because I had a trampolining
competition, or some other commitment. But I also felt
nervous about going, and preferred to stay at home. With
hindsight I can see that this might have looked like rude-
ness, as though I didn't care and wasn't even prepared
to try to join in with the family, though it actually had
a lot more to do with my nervousness and feeling that
I was an outsider.

A couple of days into the holiday Josh asked me, 'Why
don't you ever come up to see us? I hear that you don't
want to come.' His manner was confrontational and I felt
cornered. I mumbled that it was simply that I'd had sporting

commitments. But the whole incident left me very upset. Normally I never questioned or confronted Julie and Paul. But this time I felt so upset that I went to Julie and said, 'Why did you tell Josh that I didn't want to go and see them?' Julie didn't answer. She just looked at me. I told her what Josh had said, but she simply refused to answer me and was very dismissive of the whole thing. I walked away and went back on my own to our chalet. I was frustrated and hurt.

That evening I was brushing my teeth in the bathroom when Paul flung open the door and started shouting at me: 'How dare you speak to my wife like that? I won't have you living with us any longer.' By this time his face was red and his eyes were bulging and I thought he was going to hit me.

I fled to my room. I felt terrified and distraught and was in tears. I didn't feel I had been rude to Julie, yet because of what I had said it appeared that they would refuse to have me any longer. Through the thin wall I could hear Julie and Paul talking in their room. Paul's voice was loud enough for me to hear him saying, 'That's it, she's going.'

The next day, when I got up, they had all left the chalet. I had no idea where they were. Had they simply gone to the slopes, ahead of me? I set off to find the ski school where the children had lessons. I thought that if I could find them I would find out where everyone was meeting for lunch.

It took me ages to do the rounds of the many ski schools.

After some time I found the right one but the instructor said the Minters weren't there. I was worried. Where could they have gone? Were they doing this to punish me? Was I so awful that they refused to be around me, or even to tell me where they were?

I skied alone for a while but I lost my way. When I got my bearings again I went back to the chalet to wait. Eventually they all returned. They had been for a day out, but they said absolutely nothing to me about their day or mine – they simply carried on as normal.

They didn't ask me to leave, but things became even more strained between us. I never got over Paul's outburst and I could no longer bear to be in the same room as him. I spent even more time in my room, or out if I could find somewhere to go. I felt alienated and rejected.

Julie barely spoke to me any more, and to my distress she announced that she would no longer be driving me to my trampoline club. Until then she had taken me to the club two or three times a week, after school. It was a fairly long way, about fifty minutes' drive. Julie would go off and do some shopping while I was in the club, and then she'd collect me and take me home.

While I know it must have been an effort for her to do this, trampolining was a hugely important part of my life, which Julie had known about from the start. Most kids do activities of some kind after school, and their parents take them. Now the lifts were to end.

I managed to get to the club on my own, taking buses,

but it took for ever. My instructor, Mike, realising I was
making a long journey, sometimes gave me a lift home,
which helped. But apart from the difficulty I now had in
getting to the club, it hurt me very much that Julie wouldn't
take me. I felt that she was punishing me.

I was now learning to drive with the father of a friend
from trampolining, and I enjoyed the lessons. I was able
to pay for them from money from the sale of our house,
which had been put into trust for me after my mother's
death. It was this money that paid for all my 'extras' like
school trips, holidays, and the driving lessons. Whenever I
needed to pay for something I went to see the solicitor who
held the funds in trust and explained to him what I wanted
money for. If he felt it was appropriate, he would give me
permission. Since I never asked for anything extravagant
there was usually no problem.

In the summer term I took my GCSEs again, hoping I'd
done better this time. It had been hard going, but I wanted
to pass well enough to give myself the option of doing A-
levels.

In the meantime the summer holidays loomed and I
wondered how I would get through them. I was living with
a family who didn't want me and I had no one who did,
and nowhere to go. Day after day I thought about killing
myself. I felt there was absolutely no reason to stay alive.
This was an almost permanent state for me, but hadn't
been helped by the rejection I felt from the Minters. I had
my friends, who were lovely. But friendship alone wasn't

enough to overcome my deep despair, or to fill the hole left in my life by the absence of a family and the trauma I had been through.

My hopelessness was a reflection of what was going on inside me, and how I saw myself and my life. A couple of years later, John Buss, a GP who became a good friend, said to me, 'It's all about your perception.' Although I didn't understand it at the time, much later I came to see how true this was. I perceived my life as pointless and hopeless, and this would only change when I was able to perceive it in a different way. The change had to come from inside me.

But at sixteen, I could only see that life was pointless without the love of a family. Dying seemed a much better prospect than staying in a world that didn't want me.

My fearful and unhappy state was compounded by an incident which happened when I was visiting Nan one day. While I was sitting with her in the living room, I saw my father walk in through the front gate. He had come back early – no doubt intending to force me to see him. I felt absolute panic. I jumped to my feet and ran upstairs, locking myself in the bathroom where I sat on the floor, curled into a ball and trembling violently, until Nan came and called through the door: 'It's all right, he's gone.' Eventually I unlocked the door and came downstairs, still trembling.

I left the house, terrified that he was waiting for me outside, and knew that I could never go back, which meant I would lose Nan too. My father hadn't just taken away my mother – he had taken away so many of the other people I cared about.

At this stage I barely ever saw my brother and sister or any other relatives. I felt they had all been taken from me through my father's actions. I occasionally heard news of Sarah and John through Gran. When I went round to Gran's I would always ask how Sarah and John were, and Gran would say: 'It's nice that you ask, because they never do.' It hurt me to hear that. I used to leave them Christmas and birthday cards and for a few years Sarah left cards for me too, although later, for some reason, she stopped.

Both Sarah and John were getting on with their lives as best they could. I did visit John, once or twice, after phoning him. He was pleasant, but we found very little to say to one another and seeing him only confirmed for me that he and Sarah really were lost to me.

In the end each one of us was struggling with grief and loss, and we did it separately because we had no idea how to do it together. Our grandparents, who could have been the link and held us together, were not able to.

The person I had come to trust most was Chris, my social worker. It had taken a long time for me to trust her, but Chris was consistent and made it clear that for her my interests came first. She had never pushed me to talk about anything, and only ever showed incredible patience. Because of this, I made the decision to confide in her that my father had sexually abused me. She would be the first person I had ever told about it and before I did so I asked her if I could tell her something that she would never tell anyone else. She explained that she would have to ask her boss for permission to keep such a secret. She did, and when she came back to me and said yes, she could keep it private, I told her. I said only one sentence – it was all I could manage. But after so many years of holding everything inside, it was a huge thing for me. Chris didn't hug me: she was probably cautious about doing the wrong thing, although a hug might have been just what I needed. But she said, 'I'm so sorry that happened to you, as well as everything else.'

I appreciated her kindness, and wished I had felt better for telling her. But I didn't. It had been a huge effort, and still I was nowhere near to being ready to truly open up or express all the feelings and thoughts that haunted me.

Burdened by these thoughts and feelings, by the endless sense of rejection that I still felt and by my loneliness and isolation, I reached a point, once again, where I felt I couldn't go on. I often thought about my mother and dreamed of being with her again. If I died I *could* be with her. My life seemed hopeless: I was broken and unable to believe that there would ever be anything to live for.

One Saturday afternoon, shortly after I had retaken my GCSEs, and soon after that visit to Nan's when my father had appeared, I decided once more to end it all. Julie and Paul had taken Dominic and Daisy out and I was alone in the house. I got out the Anadin tablets I had been hoarding and managed to swallow about thirty of them before I began to choke and simply couldn't get any more down.

I lay on my bed, hoping that I could just die, peacefully and quickly. But half an hour later a terrible thought occurred to me. I realised that when the family came back, one of the children might come in and find me. I hadn't thought of that before, but the idea was unbearable. I knew I couldn't put them through that and I began to panic.

By this time I was feeling very sick. I couldn't phone Suzie, as I knew she had gone away, so I tried another friend who lived quite close. Her younger sister answered and said that my friend wasn't in. The third person I tried was my dance teacher, Leila, who was also a friend of Julie and Paul's and who lived nearby.

When Leila answered I said, 'I've done something, please come round.' Hearing the panic in my voice, she told me to wait there and came straight round with her young daughter Vicky. When she arrived and saw how ill I was she sent Vicky up to play in Daisy's room and then called her husband Bill and an ambulance.

Bill arrived just before the ambulance did, and it was he who accompanied me to the William Harvey Hospital in Ashford. He was a local headmaster and I knew him: he and Leila only lived five minutes away and were good friends of the Minters. Leila said to me, 'I'm not very good at dealing with this sort of thing, so it's best that Bill does it. I'll drop Vicky off with a friend and then catch up with you at the hospital.' I didn't mind – I was just glad to have someone with me, and Bill was calm and reassuring.

In the accident-and-emergency cubicle where I was taken the medical staff seemed impatient and very detached and clinical. Perhaps they thought a teenager who'd taken an overdose was just time-wasting. It certainly felt that way. They made me drink a ghastly black drink with charcoal in it, to line my stomach and make me sick. I only managed to get half the drink down, but it worked – I was very, very sick.

Bill stayed with me throughout, while Leila, who arrived a little later, waited outside. Once I had thrown up the contents of my stomach I was moved to a ward, and Leila came in to see me. 'We'll wait with you until Julie and Paul get here, however long that takes,' she promised. I trusted what she had said and appreciated it. I knew they were putting themselves out for me, or perhaps for the Minters, since they were such good friends. Either way, I was very glad not to be left alone.

When Julie finally arrived, Leila and Bill left. I knew they had assumed that Julie would stay with me. But she clearly had no intention of staying. 'I've just come to check that you're all right,' she told me. 'I've got to go.' Her manner was cold and the hurt I felt was huge. Of course she was upset, and I realised she must have taken my actions as a rejection of her and her family. But it wasn't – it was a cry for help, and all I wanted was for her to take my hand and say, 'Why did you do it?' Even an angry response from her would have been preferable. But there was nothing but cool indifference. She nodded to me, turned and left. Her entire visit had lasted no more than three minutes.

After Julie had gone I lay in bed, my stomach aching and nauseous. I was feeling bitterly hurt and alone. A little later Chris arrived, and I was touched, because she wasn't on duty and had come in her own time. She was kind and concerned and stayed with me for a while, promising to come back the next day.

Suzie also came to visit me the following day, bringing my favourite sweets: red laces. Perhaps because of the link with my mother that sweets gave me because of the Rolos, I loved them, and while I found regular food hard to get down I could eat a lot of confectionery.

I could see that Suzie was upset. 'When Mum told me what you'd done I burst into tears,' she said. It had affected her deeply and I realised that she really cared about me and felt that perhaps she hadn't been a good enough friend. In fact she'd been a great friend, listening quietly when I told her how unhappy I was at Julie and Paul's, accepting what I said without arguing or trying to talk me out of it, and being very supportive. My suicide attempt, she said, had made her understand just how unhappy I was. I was grateful: she could have run away or said she couldn't deal with it, but she didn't.

Neither Julie nor Paul came to see me after that first brief visit of Julie's. Quite possibly they felt upset and let down by me, and perhaps they also felt they had failed as carers. But it was hard for me to be in the hospital alone, so I was very glad of Chris and Suzie, who both came again.

Then, two days after I had been admitted, I was lying in bed in my small side ward when I heard a familiar voice, just outside the doors, saying, 'Hello, my name's Tom Sanders, I've come to see my daughter Gayle.'

I have no idea who had told him I was there, or what had happened. He shouldn't have known, and he certainly shouldn't have come to the hospital, as he wasn't supposed to make contact with me.

I jumped out of the bed and hid underneath it. A doctor come over and, seeing how scared I was, pulled the curtains around my bed. His manner was kind and considerate as he told me that my father had arrived and asked if I wanted to see him. I couldn't speak, but I managed to shake my head.

'That's OK,' he said, 'you don't need to see him. And if ever you want to talk to me, just tell one of the nurses.' He went back outside and sent my father away, but once again he had come close to me and all the horror and fear had been brought back.

I was touched by the doctor's kindness, but I never did talk to him. Kind as he was, he was a stranger, and I was no nearer to being able to talk about how I felt, to him or to anyone else.

A couple of days later I was sent home. On my first evening back in the house, Julie went out. Paul was there and his manner seemed to have softened. He asked if he could get me anything and he was a little gentler towards me than he'd been in the past. But it was a different story with Julie who, when I saw her the next day, was distant and cool with me. She was clearly angry about what I had done, but she didn't talk to me about it or ask me anything. Instead it was almost as if she had completely distanced herself from me.

That night I couldn't sleep. I knew it was going to be impossible for me to stay with the Minters after this. What on earth was going to happen to me next?

15

A *tentative start*

It was Dr Hayter who put to me the two grim choices that
the authorities had come up with. After my suicide attempt
it was clear that neither the Minters nor social services felt
it was appropriate for me to stay in that household.

'Gayle, you really need help,' Dr Hayter said. Then she
told me that I could either stay in the local hospital's psychiatric wing or go back to Beech House, St Augustine's adolescent unit.

I was horrified. Surely they couldn't send me back there?
It had been three years since I'd left, but I still shuddered
when I thought of that bleak place. I couldn't bear the
thought of going back to it. But I knew that the local
psychiatric ward would almost certainly be worse.

Desperate for a way out, I asked whether it would be
possible for me to attend Beech House during the day, while
continuing to live at Julie and Paul's place. To my relief,
after some consultations among those concerned with my
case, it was agreed that I could. I was to attend Beech

House seven days a week, from nine a.m. until five p.m., but I could go back to the Minters' home at night.

It wasn't much of a compromise, but it was better than being at Beech House full-time. The summer holidays were about to start, and I was leaving Brockhill School, so it was agreed that I would attend Beech House for the summer while the search resumed for new foster-parents. Although I was now seventeen I was still the responsibility of social services, and would remain so until I reached my eighteenth birthday.

A car was organised to drive me to and from the unit each day, and it was with some trepidation that I stepped back into Beech House on that first morning. It was the last place on earth I wanted to be.

It was still mostly as awful as when I'd been a resident, although some good changes had been made. Then the place had been chaotic, with all kinds of organisational problems, an atmosphere of aggression and regular outbreaks of violence from the patients. Now it seemed calmer and far better organised. Someone had obviously made changes, and they were a definite improvement. Not that it made me want to be there any more than before. I still hated it and knew that it wasn't the right place for me. In a small, nurturing therapeutic centre I might have been helped, but Beech House was just too big, impersonal and institutional.

The adolescent unit didn't take day patients, so I was an oddity from the start. The other teenagers couldn't understand what I was doing there and I got the impression that the staff didn't want me around. But, as had been the case so many times before in my life, I had no option.

Of course, all the other patients I had known before were long gone, though some of the staff were still the same. Now I was the oldest teenager in the unit, which felt very different. I spent my days watching television, playing pool and chatting with the other patients while waiting to hear what would happen to me next. I saw the psychiatrist every now and then, but we made no progress because I still felt unable to talk about anything that had happened to me. I also had to join in the post-breakfast morning group, which was still part of the daily routine. I reverted to the two-sentence reply I had used in the past: 'My day yesterday was OK. That's all I have to say.' I really couldn't see the point of me being there, and only hoped that it wouldn't be for too long.

Annie, the unit's social worker, had moved jobs and was no longer there. I had seen her once or twice during the past three years, but not often. I was sad that she had left Beech House, because she had been one of the few people there with whom I felt comfortable. I'd liked being able to go to her for a cuddle or just to sit with her for a while in her office. Now there was no one among the staff at the unit that I could relate to in the same way.

While my days at Beech House seemed pointless, my evenings were worse. At Julie and Paul's home things were

extremely uncomfortable and awkward. We all knew that
my placement with them hadn't worked and I would be
leaving, and none of us really knew what to say, or how
to behave with each other. I felt let down and rejected by
them, and they probably felt out of their depth and frustrated by me. Julie was still very distant and never spoke
to me unless she had to, while Paul tried harder but still
couldn't hide his awkwardness around me. To avoid being
with them I either sat alone in my room or went over to
see Suzie. Her family were as nice as Louise's had been,
and her home was a welcome refuge for me during that
uncertain summer.

A few weeks into this new routine, Chris came to see
me with a proposal. 'Annie has offered to foster you,' she
told me. 'Would you consider it?' I was surprised. How
had this happened? Chris explained that she had met Annie
recently and had told her what I was now doing. Annie
had come back to Chris a few days later, and said that she
and her husband would like to foster me and would I like
to go and meet her family?

I should have felt pleased and happy. Annie was a lovely
person, someone I had felt comfortable with, someone who
had shown me kindness and patience. And inasmuch as I
could feel anything, I was pleased. But at this point in my
life I was almost unable to feel. I was a lost girl, just going
through the motions of life, managing to breathe and eat
and sleep, but inwardly broken. I had been so hurt, so traumatised and so abandoned that I no longer believed

anything good could ever happen to me. I didn't know how to trust, how to hope, how to feel joy. All I knew was hurt and fear and dread. And all I expected was rejection, criticism and disappointment.

So I said yes to meeting Annie's family again – I had met them once briefly at Beech House when I was thirteen. But I didn't feel hope or excitement or optimism. I just did as I had to do.

I met the family at their home in Canterbury. Annie's husband John was a lecturer in philosophy at the University of Kent, while since she had left Beech House Annie had been working as a lecturer in social services at Kent's other university. They had two adopted children, Faizal, who was eleven and Ayesha, who was seven.

From the moment I stepped inside their house I knew that theirs was a warm, loving and very open family. They welcomed me without any formality, and I felt that this was a place where I could live. I was still extremely wary and was conscious that things could go wrong. But I was also grateful that they would even consider having me in their home and I gladly agreed to go and live with them.

The one condition that Annie insisted on was that I should start psychotherapy, once or possibly even twice a week. I knew that she believed it would help me, so I said I would, even though I didn't want to do it and it felt like a huge imposition. I still wasn't ready – or able – to talk, so I knew there would be little point in me seeing someone.

But I respected Annie's request and appreciated that I needed to meet her halfway.

Annie and her family were going to their house in France for the last part of the summer holiday, and they invited me to join them there. That was still a couple of weeks away – the formalities of my placement still had to be sorted out. And in the meantime Chris told me that she was leaving social services.

This was sad news. Chris had been one of the few constants in my life for the past five years and she meant a lot to me. I had always been struck by her commitment and patience towards me. I also appreciated her willingness not to push me. In addition to this I knew that she had also had to deal with my father and his endless demands for meetings, reports on me from social services and so on in his attempt to get what he wanted. She did this with one priority in mind – to protect me. I knew that, and I had come to trust her and care a lot for her.

Chris promised me that she would always keep in touch with me, but I wasn't sure I could believe her, simply because I couldn't imagine anyone really caring about me and wanting to stay in contact. Even though I knew how reliable she was and that for me she had always gone beyond the professional requirements of her role, I couldn't imagine why she would want to make the effort to communicate with me once she didn't have to. So it was with a heavy heart that I said goodbye to her, shortly before I packed up my few possessions into suitcases and cardboard boxes, ready to move to Annie's place.

A week or two before I left the Minters I got my GCSE results. I had passed all eight that I'd taken, with reasonable grades, and although I had very little idea of what I was going to do with my life I was pleased. It meant I could go on to take A-levels at the new school Annie had suggested for me.

In late August, having recently passed my driving test, I drove over to leave my things in Annie's house. Then Paul drove me to the airport to board a flight to France. I sat on the plane, looking out at the Channel and wondering what lay ahead of me. I was grateful to have left Beech House. And I was also relieved to be moving, although I would miss Dominic and Daisy.

I had felt very rejected by Julie Minter, but I can see that perhaps she also felt rejected by me. She and Paul had done their best, but it had never really worked out. Would things be any better at Annie's? And would I be able to move forward with my life?

The family's French home was in Valros, a small, quaint and very pretty village in the south of France. Here they had a house big enough for all of them, including Annie's mother Norah and me too.

From the beginning I never felt as though I was imposing on the family, and this meant a great deal to me. With the Minters I had always somehow felt that I was in the way and that the family were doing me a favour, but would truthfully rather I wasn't there. With Annie's family it was different.

First there was Annie herself. In her late forties, with red hair and bags of energy, Annie was a warm, perceptive and bright woman. She already knew me and knew all about my past. She had even met my father and it was a huge relief to me that I didn't need to try to explain anything. Most important of all, Annie was not a friend or crony of my father's. The opposite was true: she had no time for him and her main concern was to help me and to keep me safe.

Knowing that there would be no split loyalties, no hidden agenda and no chance of my father ringing up for a chat one day made an enormous difference to me. And so did the fact that Annie's family managed to absorb me without any apparent ripples in their normal routine. They all simply carried on doing things just as they had before, so I never felt as though I was putting them out.

I knew Annie, but I needed to know what her husband John was like. He was the unknown quantity for me, and initially I was wary and cautious. But I soon discovered that John was a lovely man. He was one of those people who was comfortable with himself. He cooked a lot, chatted, read, played with the kids and was very easy to be around. And, because he behaved perfectly normally with me, I felt safe with him. I also enjoyed his quirky and creative nature, which was apparent from the beginning. And he was the least judgmental man I had ever met.

I liked the children very much, but then I had always got on better with children than with adults. Faizal was delighted that I was happy to play bat and ball on the beach with him and Ayesha was very accepting of this new person in their midst, as small children so often are. I also got on with Norah. She was seventy-eight and had a clear, bright mind, and I enjoyed sitting and talking to her.

However, despite this generous, friendly family welcoming me so warmly, I didn't find it easy being with them. I didn't really know how to be part of a family: I was so used to being on the outside, and to shutting myself away for fear of intruding. I felt awkward and, at times, overwhelmed. But even when these feelings were difficult to manage I was aware that I'd rather be with this family than anywhere else I had been since my mother's death.

After a couple of weeks we all travelled back to their house in Canterbury to prepare for the new school and university term.

The family's home was very lived-in and full of photographs and colour – on cushions, sofas and walls. There was a big living room, with a Liberty-print sofa in the middle, and a big kitchen, with a large table where everyone ate.

There was always noise and activity. Both the children were bright and very active. Faizal watched all the football matches he could, and kept all the scores in an exercise book. Ayesha played the piano, and when she wasn't playing it she was singing at the top of her lungs. Her friend Phoebe, who lived over the road, was always in the house and the two of them would laugh and chatter away.

As well as all of us humans there were two cats, Rosie and Jojo, which Ayesha adored and called her babies. And visitors and friends often popped in. When he wasn't at work, where he was the kind of lecturer who students would come to for both academic and emotional help, John was either shopping or in the kitchen cooking enormous meals for everyone. Annie, meanwhile, worked incredibly hard. She was now lecturing by day and working as a psychotherapist in the evenings. She also supervised the counsellors at a rape line phone-in service.

In amongst this menagerie I had my own spacious, airy room at the top of the house. I liked being at the top, not because I was a teenager and wanted to get away from everyone, but because it felt safe to be tucked away up there. This was where I unpacked my boxes of sporting trophies, my clothes and my few books and ornaments and did my best to settle down to this new phase of my life.

A few days later I joined the sixth form at Chaucer Technology School to do A-levels in dance, English, sports studies and sociology. It was a mixed school which was close to Annie and John's home. Annie had felt I would be better off in a school with a more structured environment than in a sixth-form college, where the approach was more relaxed.

I was doing my dance studies out of school, with my

old dance teacher Leila. After my overdose I had carried on attending her classes. I liked her and she was an excellent teacher, but there was a little bit of awkwardness between us. I think she wasn't sure how to respond to me and probably felt protective of Julie and Paul, who were her friends.

I found school very difficult. I didn't want to go there, and I only did so because I knew it was what I should do. It wasn't easy for me starting somewhere new, and it was made worse because I was a year older than all the others. I felt very intimidated by the place and the people and found it difficult to respond to anyone. At one point in my first few days there I stood in the middle of the common room looking at all the other students and feeling totally overwhelmed. It must have showed, because a friendly-looking girl called Jo came up to me and said, 'Hello, would you like to come and sit with us?' I said, 'No, thank you,' but she came back and tried again and eventually I went over and sat with her and a couple of her friends and tried to join in.

Jo and I did become friends, and I got to know a few other students too. Having friends in my life was very important to me. With them I came the closest I could to feeling normal and ordinary, which was what I wanted. They confided in me and, although I couldn't talk to them about the bigger issues I struggled with, I did confide in them about my day-to-day life.

But while these friendships were strong, I still found it very difficult to concentrate on my studies. Whether I was socialising or studying, I would often be transfixed by a memory or a terrible thought and begin to feel panicky and anxious. Although I would attempt to continue with what I was doing, I wasn't really there: anxiety had taken over and I simply couldn't take in what I was supposed to be doing or saying.

The truth was that although I was now living with a genuinely accepting family, and my life appeared to be more stable than during all of the previous five years, I was still emotionally lost. I was no more able to grieve for Mum than I had been when she died. Life so far had been about survival for me, and I was so anxious all the time that just breathing and eating demanded an effort which at times felt almost beyond me.

At the same time as I began in my new school, I began the psychotherapy sessions that I had agreed to as a condition of my being at Annie's home. John took me to see the first woman, but she was very intense and formal and I knew she was not someone I could get on with, so I said no.

The next woman I was introduced to was nicer, but I still felt she was not my sort. Once again she was very intense, which I didn't like. I had hoped for someone more light-hearted and relaxed. However, this time, knowing that I had to see someone, I agreed to go ahead.

The staff at Beech House had asked lots of questions, but this woman didn't. And she didn't explain anything about how it was all supposed to work. I had to see her for two hour-long sessions a week and – just as had happened with Dr Hayter in the past – we spent them in silence. They were a complete waste of time for both of us.

It felt almost comical when, weeks after our sessions had begun, she finally said, 'Gayle, I'm sensing that you are finding it difficult to talk.' The next thing she said was: 'I'm just going to think about the night your mother was killed and be with you.' She closed her eyes for a while, then opened them and said, 'I can really feel your pain.'

I didn't know whether to laugh or cry at this patronising and insulting performance. She clearly had no idea what to do with me, which was a shame because a good child psychotherapist, used to dealing with trauma, can offer a lot to a distressed young person. They would certainly never launch bluntly into a subject as difficult as the violent death of a parent but would get to know the child over time, and earn their trust by talking about safe subjects such as interests and activities. If she had asked me about sport I might have been able to talk to her.

It was during the period when I was seeing her that I had an accident which deeply upset me. I was due to compete in the trampoline national finals when, during practice the evening before, I somersaulted in the air and, instead of landing on the trampoline, came down on the floor of the gym. My knee was in agony and I knew I had damaged it badly. I was taken to hospital, where I learned that I had broken my kneecap.

My leg was put in plaster from thigh to ankle, which meant I couldn't walk, let alone play sports. I was told it would have to stay on for eight weeks, after which I would need physiotherapy. No one could tell me whether I would be able to use the trampoline and reach the same high standard again.

This left me feeling very depressed. I couldn't get about on my own and had to spend a lot of time at home, inactive. A friend used to drive me to school and to the therapy sessions, where I had to sit on the floor because I couldn't manage a chair with my leg in plaster.

My knee did heal at last, though it took several months. And I was able to get back on a trampoline and eventually compete at national level again. Though I could not, now, hope to fulfil the potential I had had before the accident.

In the meantime, after six months of therapy I went in one day and said to the therapist, 'I'm not coming any more.' She said, 'OK' – and that was it.

I told Annie that the sessions weren't working and I didn't want to go again and she accepted that. It was a relief that she didn't insist that I should see someone else, though I knew she would have liked me to.

At the time I didn't know if I would *ever* be ready to open up. My feeling was: 'No one's going to force me to talk.' But looking back I can see that I needed to feel safe and nurtured before I could possibly start to explore the horrors of my past. And the therapist whom I'd been seeing most recently had no idea how to help me feel safe.

Meanwhile there was one person I did feel happy about seeing. Chris had been true to her word and was regularly in touch. In fact, when Annie moved on to a job managing a sexual abuse project for the National Children's Homes, Chris took over her old job lecturing at the university close to where we lived. I used to look forward to going over and meeting her for a coffee after school.

Life with Annie's family was infinitely better than it had been with the Minters. There was a great deal of warmth and no pressure. And that was important, because my anxiety wasn't going to disappear overnight, even with nice people around me.

16

Still broken

It was around this time that I made another very good friend. Because John worked at the university, his family, including me, were entitled to use the university medical centre. I went along to see a GP there when I was having trouble sleeping. At first I saw a lovely woman GP who was supportive and kind. She gave me tablets to help me sleep, and asked me to come back regularly, perhaps so that she could keep a general eye on me. After a while she went on maternity leave and suggested that I might like to see her colleague John Davison.

From the start Dr Davison was an enormous support to me. He could see that I was depressed and unhappy and he went out of his way to help, often spending half an hour or even an hour with me, despite the fact that appointments were meant to last no more than ten minutes. He talked many things through with me and always encouraged me to pursue my education. He used to say to me, 'It's all about your perception' and while I didn't understand that then, I have since come to appreciate how true it always is, of almost any situation.

Dr Davison was a friend of Annie's and he and his wife sometimes came to dinner. I got to know them well and even after this kind man retired from practice we stayed friends. In later years I used to visit their house in France, which was not far from Annie and John's.

I still wasn't eating much, but no one made an issue of it. They knew that I would eat when I was finally able to feel really safe. John made meals for everyone and I was free to join in or not, as I chose. They didn't always sit down together in the evenings, because everyone was so busy, so it wasn't obvious if I didn't eat. Annie gently encouraged me to, but John said nothing – he just let me know that food was there if I wanted it. They bought things I liked to eat, like yogurts, which they put in the fridge for me to help myself to. And they bought my favourite yogurt gums and kept them in a drawer so that I could help myself – the only condition being that I should do it after Ayesha was in bed so that she wouldn't eat them all.

While I did my best to settle into life with Annie and her family, and was grateful for the home they had given me, I still felt deeply unhappy and often suicidal. Even the kindness of the people around me couldn't wipe out the loss of my mother and the legacy of hurt and rejection and hopelessness of the past years. I felt that my life was a mess and found it impossible to see the point of carrying on, because I still couldn't imagine a future for myself, or believe that there would ever be anyone who would love and accept me.

I was not enjoying school at all. Although I liked the friends I had made there, I couldn't concentrate on my studies and found it difficult to manage the intensity of A-level work. I dropped sports studies early on, and this helped a little, but I still struggled with the English and sociology. And while my knee was healing I missed the dance classes with Leila, and my trampolining.

In February 1992, six months after I had moved in with Annie's family, I had my eighteenth birthday. I was on a skiing trip with the school – paid for, like other extras, from the money I had been awarded after Mum's death. I really enjoyed skiing, and the teachers accompanying us got me a birthday cake, while back at Annie's the family gave me presents and held a little celebration. I appreciated the trouble they had taken, but it was impossible for me to have any sense of being special, even on my birthday. I was becoming more and more withdrawn and the life going on around me seemed like a blur which had very little to do with me.

My contact with my family at this stage was non-existent, apart from the occasional visit to Gran and Grandad that was always initiated by me. I had not seen Nan since my suicide attempt the previous summer, prompted in part by seeing my father while I'd been at her house. It hadn't been her fault, but I simply couldn't go there again and gradually we lost touch.

Ironically, while I longed to have contact with the rest of the family, who didn't want it with me, the one person who *did* pursue me was my father. Despite becoming a vicar and taking over his own parish, and in defiance of the social-services injunction banning him from contacting me, he had never given up trying to get in touch with me. Once he was no longer able to send me letters through Nan he found other ways to get them to me. Not often, and I never read them, but the sight of his handwriting on an envelope was enough to bring back all the fear and anxiety that he always awoke in me.

After the two occasions on which he had followed me while I was at the Minters', I hoped he would give up. It was quite clear that I wanted nothing to do with him. So I was horrified when, out in Canterbury one day, I once again saw my father in his car. He was sitting behind the wheel of the parked vehicle, watching me. I saw his white dog collar and even as I felt the familiar cold clench of fear I was struck by the irony of this man supposedly being a man of God.

My own car was nearby, and once again I hurried away from him and drove rapidly home. I was badly shaken. He always seemed to know where I was and what I was doing. I couldn't bear to think of him following me any longer. I had to do something.

When I had revealed to Chris that my father had sexually abused me throughout most of my early childhood, she had suggested that I might want to prosecute him. At the time I didn't, but now I began to wonder if that might deter him. I spoke to Chris and to Annie about it, and both of them were supportive about the idea, whilst warning me that it might be too late for a prosecution.

I did go to the police, who were sympathetic and began an investigation during which they contacted not only my father but my brother and sister too and, I imagine, the doctors to whom I had been taken as a child. I gave a statement but, still feeling ambivalent about whether I wanted to go ahead, it was not as clear as it could have been. Eventually I was told that there simply was not enough evidence to go on for a prosecution. Everyone else had, of course, denied all knowledge of the abuse, so it was my word alone.

The case fizzled out and, in some strange way, I didn't mind. I had done it because I felt I should, but I hadn't really wanted to do it. The whole thing had felt too exposing and intimidating. Although it meant that my father got away with it, I knew that I simply couldn't have faced the ordeal of a court case in which I would have had to give detailed and intimate evidence against him about events I had struggled to block from my mind.

But there was another route I could take to warn him off. As the social-services injunction had lapsed when I turned eighteen, Annie suggested that I should go and see a solicitor and take out a personal injunction against my father. I did so, and was told that an injunction would mean that I would have to give evidence in court. I didn't want to do this, but the solicitor suggested an alternative: if my father agreed to it he could give the court an undertaking not to contact me, and for this I would only need to submit a short statement, prepared with the solicitor. The solicitor arranged to contact my father to find out whether he would consent to this. But he warned me that, like most legal processes, it might take some time.

During the summer holidays that year, Annie and the family went again to France. They wanted me to go with them, but I refused. I was in a bad way, and I felt too divorced from everyone and everything to feel able to join in a family summer holiday. So I stayed at home and a friend of Annie's who was working on her thesis moved into the house. She was a pleasant woman, and Annie had probably asked her to keep an eye on me, but mostly we went our own ways and didn't spend time together.

A couple of weeks into the summer I once again reached the point of no return. There wasn't a particular trigger – it was just that I thought about suicide every day and a time came when I felt I simply had to do it. I wanted to die, to end the awful, miserable effort of living when there was nothing to live for. I had been thinking for many weeks of taking another overdose and eventually the day came when I couldn't stop myself any longer.

This time I took beta blockers that had been given to me by a doctor to help with my nervousness during trampoline and dance competitions. These are drugs that are usually used for heart complaints and high blood pressure but are also sometimes used by musicians and sportsmen and women for performance-related anxiety. Their effect is to lower the blood pressure and slow the heart rate: an overdose could easily be fatal.

I took about twenty-five pills – more than enough to kill me. I waited until I was alone in the house and then swallowed them and went to bed.

The likelihood is that the woman staying in the house would have been the one to find me. She would have been concerned when she didn't see me the next day, and would have come looking for me. But as I lay waiting for the pills to act I had visions of Annie's children running upstairs when they came home in a week's time, and finding me. This wasn't logical, but I couldn't let the image go, and I began to panic.

In my mind I veered between wanting to die and feeling that perhaps I should tell someone what I'd done and try to live. Although I felt that I didn't care whether I died or not, I think I also wanted people to know how bad I felt and that I needed help.

In the end the impulse to live won against my longing for oblivion. I rang a teacher from school, Mrs Austen, whom I liked. She had never taught me, but she had been on the ski trip earlier in the year and I'd got to know her a little then. She came straight round and took me to hospital, where I had to endure having my stomach pumped.

It was a hideous ordeal. I was put on my side and a thick tube was forced down my throat and into my stomach, causing me to retch violently. A funnel was inserted in the end of the tube and water was poured in. As the liquid filled my innards I felt them stretching. Eventually the sheer volume of water entering my stomach pushed its contents back up the tube. This barbaric and excruciating process continued until the medical staff were satisfied that they had got all the pills out. While I knew it had to be done, it was one of the worst experiences I have ever had and as I was enduring it I felt terrified about what I had done to myself.

They couldn't be certain how much of the drug I had absorbed, so I was taken to a heart ward and kept on a monitor. A drip was inserted into my arm – I have no idea what it contained – and I was closely watched. I felt terrible: shaky, jerky and disorientated. In addition I had a bad reaction to whatever drug they were giving me. I felt terribly ill and wondered if I would fully recover.

Mrs Austen had stayed with me until I was moved to the ward, and she visited me every day. After three days they told me I could leave, but only if there was someone to look after me. Mrs Austen asked me if I'd like to go and stay at her house, and I did, remaining with her until Annie returned three or four days later.

Annie had been informed about what had happened and when she arrived back she was very upset. Why hadn't I been able to tell her how bad I felt, she asked. I had no answer, other than to say that I simply couldn't. I felt very sad and guilty that I had upset her so badly. I cared a lot for Annie and didn't want to hurt her.

The worst part of it all was that I still felt suicidal and

knew I couldn't trust myself not to attempt another over-dose. I didn't want to do that to Annie or her family, so I made the decision to move out. I felt that I was a burden on the family and that wasn't fair. I wished I had been able to feel differently. I didn't want Annie to feel she had failed with me. But I simply couldn't find my way out of the hopelessness I felt.

By the time I had arrived at Annie's I was a broken person, and her family's warmth and kindness, wonderful as it was, couldn't put me back together. I had simply never recovered from the double blow of losing my mother and then being abandoned by my family. The time after my mother's death could have been so different for me if someone from my family had arrived the next day and told me they would take care of me. Although I'm sure I would have had problems, and would never have got over Mum's death, if there had been someone to love me and support me I don't believe I would have become suicidal or felt that there was no reason to live. As it was, my family's attitude wounded me so deeply that I simply couldn't find my way back to any sense of purpose about life.

Annie was very upset when I told her that I was going to leave. But she also understood, and accepted that I felt it was for the best. Mrs Austen, who lived alone, had offered me her spare room and said I could live with her as a lodger. I felt this was a safer arrangement. It gave me space and there was no pressure to be with her.

Over the summer term I had struggled even harder to

concentrate on my studies, and early in the autumn term, soon after moving out of Annie's, I decided to give up and leave school. It was a relief to stop trying to study, but I had absolutely no idea what I was going do next.

Because I had been a Ward of Court the aftercare service paid the rent for my new lodging for the first few months. And as I was now eighteen I had been given the remainder of the money held in trust that I had been awarded after Mum's death. This gave me enough to live on for a while and a little space to begin thinking about what to do next with my life. I continued to go to dance classes at Leila's and spent quite a bit of time at the school, helping to teach the younger children. I was also able to go to the trampoline club again. Although my knee was never quite as strong as it had once been, I was still able to enjoy the sport and, eventually, to compete again at a high level.

To my relief the solicitor I had contacted told me that my father had agreed to the undertaking not to contact me. But to make this undertaking legal we had to go before a judge, in court. Annie came with me, and I braced myself to get through it, but it was a dreadful ordeal. I had to sit in court, just feet away from my father, while the judge said to him: 'Do you agree to this undertaking?' and he said yes. It felt almost unbearable to be so physically close to him. My stomach was in a small, tight knot throughout and I could barely breathe.

I got through the ordeal by not looking at my father even once – there was no exchange of any sort between us and I was grateful that I didn't have to speak in court. The solicitor simply handed over my statement. Afterwards I felt no relief because I didn't believe for a moment that my father would keep to the undertaking.

Because there was a killing in our past, and because my father was now a vicar, the case was picked up by the local paper, which asked me for an interview. It was the last thing I wanted to do, but a couple of people advised me that if I really wanted my father to keep away, then this might help. So I went ahead and talked to their reporter and the story they printed was picked up by a national newspaper. I gave them an interview too, and the resulting spread in the paper, although I hated seeing it and it felt desperately exposing for me, certainly seemed to act as a deterrent to my father, because I did not hear from him or see him again.

It was a long time before I began to believe that he might really leave me alone. There were times, even years afterwards, when I looked over my shoulder fearfully, or felt a tightening in my stomach at the sight of handwriting that was similar to his. But eventually I realised that perhaps he had really given up.

I heard very little more about him after I took out the injunction and gave the interviews. But the following year I heard from Gran that he had married again – and my brother and sister had both been at the wedding. I found this very difficult to understand, and they in turn apparently found it hard to forgive me for my allegations of sexual abuse. It seemed that the final fragile threads of our relationship were breaking and I felt very sad about it.

17

Learning

My knee was now much better and I was able to be active again. For the next few months, while lodging with Mrs Austen, I filled my time with dance, trampoline, seeing friends and just walking and reading. I didn't feel ready for either a job or further education and I still felt desperate and very uncertain about the future. I felt I had to do something, but I had no idea what. I wanted to find a way to make things right for myself, and to create a life and a future that I might feel able to live for. I wanted to be able to study, and to achieve a career. But until I could do something about my inability to concentrate, study was impossible, and achieving a worthwhile life felt like trying to climb a mountain, blindfolded. I didn't know where to begin, but I knew I had to find a way forward or I would keep trying to kill myself until I succeeded. And, eventually, I took a tentative step in a positive direction.

I had often thought about Dora Black, the psychiatrist who specialised in the study of the impact of the killing of one parent by another on the children concerned. I'd felt at the time that she had an insight into how I felt. She had said things that were uncannily accurate, and that no one else had ever said to me. She knew the things I couldn't explain to anyone. I had always felt so isolated from everyone around me, because they had no idea what I was feeling. But here was a woman who did have an idea, and who could sum up in a few sentences much of what I was feeling.

I decided to write to her. I had no idea whether she could see me, or help. But it was somewhere to start. In the letter I told her that she had been the only person who seemed to understand something about me, and I asked her if she would see me again.

Writing this letter was an important step for me. It was the first time I had done something active to help myself. At this point in my life nobody was going to help me if I didn't ask for help. I was now a young adult, and no longer the responsibility of social services or anyone else. I had to begin to make a life for myself, and the letter to Dora Black was an acknowledgement that I wanted to do this.

Much to my surprise Dora responded straight away, sending me an appointment to see her in a couple of weeks' time. By now I had a little car of my own, so I drove up to London to see her.

I knew that there would be no point having this meeting if I remained silent. I had to make an effort to speak. So I told her about my suicide attempts, my depression, my inability to concentrate and my profound sense of rejection. And I told her that I wanted to find a way forward.

At the end of the session she said, 'Let me think about it' and asked me to come back a few weeks later. When I did, she explained that she couldn't see me herself, as she specialised in children and adolescents and as I was now officially an adult I came under the remit of adult services.

It felt quite shocking to realise that I was now considered to be a mature person with 'adult' problems. I still felt so young – in fact, I felt like a child. For the first time I saw that people were suddenly meant to 'grow up' and behave in a certain way. This seemed so confusing to me. It was hard to feel grown up when I had never experienced the kind of nurturing that supports a child during the time when they are becoming an adult. However, I had to accept what Dora said, and she told me that she had a male colleague, one of the best in the field of post-traumatic stress, with whom she felt I could work well. My feelings were very mixed. I was deeply frustrated that she couldn't see me herself. That was what I really wanted. But if I couldn't see her, I wasn't at all sure that I wanted to see a man. I told her this, and she said, 'I think it will do you some good.'

I wasn't happy about it but I respected her and was grateful that she had seen me. I felt that, despite the enormous resistance I felt to seeing a man, I must give her recommendation a chance.

Dora asked me to see her colleague, who was called Stuart, and then to come back and let her know how it had gone. I agreed that I would and went home, feeling very uncertain about the whole thing, to wait for an appointment with Dora's associate.

Stuart worked at the Middlesex Hospital and a few days later a letter arrived, offering me an appointment and enclosing several forms that I was asked to fill out. I found all the forms very frustrating and was on the brink of dropping the whole idea. But I felt that Dora Black had been very kind to me and I wanted to reciprocate. So I forced myself to fill in the forms and sent them back, and a couple of weeks later I went to the Middlesex for my appointment, which happened to be on my nineteenth birthday. My first impression of Stuart was of a tall, thin man who had a friendly smile and warm eyes. He asked me about some of the answers I had given on the forms, and told me he would be happy to start seeing me weekly.

My conclusion after that first meeting was that he seemed all right, though I was cautious. I went back to see Dora Black and said that I would carry on with him and see how it went, and that I would be open-minded about it. And so I began travelling weekly to the Middlesex Hospital to see Stuart. The journey there and back took me most of a day, but I had the time and I knew I had to give this a go.

It took me a while, perhaps a few months, but I began to really like Stuart, and eventually to trust him. Slowly, I started to open up to him in a way I never had with anyone else. He seemed to know when to hold back and when to push me, when to ask questions and when to wait. If I said I was wrong or blamed myself, he didn't argue with me. He simply said, 'OK, tell me how it was – what bit did you get wrong?'

In time I began to feel that he was committed to me and would be there for me no matter what. He showed me a remarkable level of support, phoning me when I was going through a particularly bad time and telling me that I could phone him if I needed to. I appreciated how human he was: I wasn't just a job to him, I was a person, and he cared. And while he often challenged me, he never judged me, and he was patient, committed and dedicated.

Seeing Stuart was the turning point for me. It wasn't that I never felt suicidal again: I did, many times. Nor was it that I felt suddenly happier, or clearer about my direction in life. My progress was slow, painfully slow at times. But what I found in Stuart was someone who would never let me down. From that first session he was always there, and the bond of trust I established with him allowed me gradually to develop a sense of self and of purpose.

For a year my main focus was on going to see Stuart. The sessions with him became my lifeline and central to everything. Gradually, once I felt complete trust in him, I was able to open up to him about what had happened in my childhood, about my parents, and about what I had gone through since my mother's death. In doing this I was able to begin to experience raw feelings of grief, sadness and loss, for the first time. With Stuart's support it felt safe, at last, to cry. The only thing I still didn't feel able to talk to him about was what had happened on the night my mother died. That would come, but it was the last and most difficult area to open up. I had closed it down so tightly inside myself that revealing it was going to be very, very hard.

I continued to lodge with Mrs Austen and to pursue a handful of activities, but now most of my energy went into my therapy. It was painfully hard to talk about things that I had kept bottled up inside for years and never spoken about. But I wanted to do it.

The following year Mrs Austen told me that she was moving, so I needed to find somewhere else to live. She told me that another teacher at the school, Mike Smith, sometimes took in lodgers, so I got in touch with him and his wife. The Smiths told me they hadn't had a lodger for ages, but agreed that I could go and meet them. When I arrived they were eating fish and chips and they invited me to join them. They had two children, Jake, nine, and Chloe, seven. I sat down and Chloe came over and sat on my lap. Mike and his wife Penny said I was very welcome to come and lodge with them and I said I'd like to, for a few months.

The Smiths turned out to be an adorable family, very warm, friendly and accepting. I lived with them as a lodger, paying rent, but they let me join in what they were doing as much or as little as I liked, which suited me well. Mike and Penny were very easygoing, and I got on very well with the children and was always happy to babysit or take them to school.

I ended up staying in their home for the next three years. They gave me a stable base from which I could come and go as I wanted, with friendship on offer but enough space for me to be alone when I needed to. It was the right formula for me, and without any pressure to fit in I became very close to the family.

I also got to know another family who lived in the same village. Joanne and Neil White were a really nice couple, with a little girl called Charlotte. Over time I became close to them, and when they had two more little girls, Ellie and Rosie, I really loved going over to see the children and play with them.

For the next couple of years I put all my energy into trying to find a way forward and get myself together. I still played sports, danced, and kept up with my friends. But the therapy with Stuart was the most important thing in my life. And it took a lot out of me: I was often drained and exhausted by the effort of looking at my past and bringing all the feelings I had held in for so long to the surface.

Eventually, largely through the therapy, I came to the decision that I wanted to pursue my education and I became determined to go to university and make a go of it. I had always felt that education was important, and had been keen to learn. It felt like something that was missing in my life. Now I wanted to give it another go, and I began to look into whether I could take a degree without having first taken my A-levels.

I was encouraged in this by John Buss, the GP who had been such a strongly supportive figure to me over the past few years. He put me in touch with a tutor at the University of Kent to see whether she could advise me on my chances of getting in.

I felt that education was a positive choice, and one I wouldn't regret. I knew that I could have chosen to take drugs or alcohol as a way of blotting out the pain I'd felt. But I also knew those would be disaster routes and I wanted to make a different choice. I felt I couldn't go wrong with education – it was something that I could rely on and that would be a good thing, no matter what else happened.

Going to university wasn't just about education, important though that was to me. I also wanted to rejoin the world of my peers. I felt that they were all getting on with their lives, while I was in limbo. I longed to be in a shared situation with people of a similar age, studying, living and enjoying ourselves together. So far I had led such a lonely existence, only joining in with my peers at a very removed level and feeling isolated and distant from their experiences. Now I wanted to be part of that journey towards adulthood and independence that others of my age were taking. I was still intermittently suicidal; those feelings hadn't disappeared altogether. But I wanted to move on, to stop feeling that way and to make a life for myself. I had reached a point in my life where, for the first time, I began to visualise some kind of personal future, sketchy though that still was.

My dreams of education were reinforced when I went to visit Suzie, several times, at her university, highlighting for me what was a normal and healthy progression in life. I enjoyed meeting her new friends, who were lovely, and seeing what her life on campus was like.

The University of Kent admissions staff told me that without A-levels I could only do a part-time degree. I didn't want that, so I went back to them and explained that I wanted to do it full-time, and eventually they agreed.

The subject I chose was social policy. I'd thought about psychology or sociology, both subjects that interested me, but what I liked about social policy was that it had a strong political element and that it related to the theory and practice of the welfare state. I wasn't sure what I wanted to do after the degree – I didn't have a career in mind – I just looked at the prospectus of the social policy degree course and thought it seemed really interesting.

I was now twenty-two and was due to begin my degree studies in the autumn of 1996. But in the meantime there was something that I knew I had to do. Although I had by now talked to Stuart a certain amount about my mother's death, I still had not really explored it. Now I felt that I wanted and needed to go into it more deeply before beginning the next phase of my life. I was still regularly having nightmares about it and I hoped that by talking about it in depth I might be able to move on. But I was also quite certain that going into the details would bring to the surface the cause of the suicidal feelings which I'd had since the age of twelve.

I thought of suicide as my best friend. That may sound strange, but the thought that I could end it all when I wanted to was comforting. It was my way of controlling my life, knowing that I could vanish from this hurtful and rejecting world. My relationship with suicide was a very close one, too close for the comfort of my friends and society in general. Few people understood my suicidal thinking, believing me to be selfish and deliberately playing with the unacceptable. But for me it was one of the very few resources I had, and sometimes only knowing that I could leave this life gave me the strength to go on living it.

I decided that I wanted to be in a safe environment, one that would care for and support me, when I finally opened up. So I asked Stuart to arrange for me to spend two months in Ticehurst House Hospital, a private psychiatric clinic. This was a place that Stuart had told me about in the past, when he had suggested that a stay there might be helpful. But at this point he was not convinced that becoming an in-patient was the best thing for me. He felt it might be better for me to stay at home, and to carry on having contact with my friends.

Despite his reservations, I wanted to go. It felt like a good, proactive decision and a way of giving myself a support system. I decided to go ahead and admit myself, feeling that if I managed to talk, then great, and if I didn't, well, at least I would have given it my best shot. I hoped I would be kept safe and nurtured therapeutically as I went through the ordeal of attempting to open up. And I would really try, because this felt like my last chance to lay the past to rest and make a fresh start.

18

A turning point

As I drove through Ticehurst's idyllic grounds, I felt very apprehensive about choosing to be an in-patient and the prospect of talking about something that had so far been locked away deep inside me.

Ten years on, the killing was still so all-encompassing and unimaginably awful in my mind that I had barely been able to touch on it in three years of therapy with Stuart. Now I was determined to make myself broach it, with the help of the Ticehurst therapists. But as I went through the motions of signing in and being shown to my room, I knew that the prospect of what lay ahead had already sent me into a very fragile suicidal state.

What I really wanted and needed was a home, with a loving parent who could support and care for me at the end of each day as I went through this ordeal. But there was no home and no parent, so in my mind Ticehurst was my substitute. I hoped the staff there would care for me in the warm and loving way that I so badly needed.

I can't remember much about those first few days at Ticehurst. In my memory it's all a blur and fairly unreachable. I saw a Jungian analyst who was very charismatic and to whom I could talk fairly easily. But although I liked his friendly and relaxed style in my sessions with him, I had not yet been able to talk about my mother's death.

My first clear memory is of a Monday afternoon, about a week after my admittance. I was in my room, resting, when I felt a strong sense of panic and unbearable pain, a pain that was emotional but so intense that it was a physical feeling too. Its depth and intensity led to an overwhelming desire to leave my body and fly away to a place of safety.

Even if there had been someone there to offer a hug or to listen, it wouldn't have helped. I recognised that desperate desire to leave myself behind – it was overwhelming and indescribable. I wanted to die because I felt that was the only way to find a place of safety and release from my lonely and pointless existence. It was, of course, a feeling I had experienced many times before, in fact on a daily basis for most of my life. But the feelings weren't any easier for me to rationalise or cope with just because I had experienced them so often in my past. It was just as frightening and lonely as it had been every other time.

The anticipation of talking about my mother's death and my own childhood was too much for me. It filled me with fear and panic. As I struggled with the intensity of the pain and desperation, I felt as if I had been doing this for an eternity. And, as had happened several times in the past, I felt I simply couldn't do it any more. I didn't have the strength to go on: I needed to end the pain, and the only way to end it was to die.

As I carefully removed the belt from my dressing gown, everything went into slow motion and my head felt numb. I had no pills to take, but this would be better, quicker and more final. I looked around the bedroom for something I could tie the cord to, something strong enough to hold my weight.

As I was searching for a secure anchor point I began to think about the people I cared for and would never see again. My friends – Annie, Chris, Stuart, the Smiths; all those who had supported me and shown me warmth and concern. But I quickly shut these thoughts out of my mind, knowing that if I thought about those I was fond of I would not be able to kill myself. And I *had* to kill myself, because I could not live any longer in this turmoil and despair. Better to convince myself that nobody cared and nobody would miss me. That in fact everyone would be better off without my burdensome depression, suicidal thoughts and endless despair over life and my non-existent future. It can't be easy trying to help and support someone who feels such hopelessness.

I spotted a place where I could tie the cord and climbed up onto the windowsill. I tied the belt to the bar above the window, and then looped it around my neck and tightened it until I could feel it pinching my skin. As I doubled the knot a few times I tightened it more, and could feel my airway blocking. As my breathing became more difficult, I felt the stinging pain and pinching of the cord around my neck. I let my legs go floppy so that I could test the strength of the belt and as I leaned my weight against it I could feel pins and needles in my head and a rushing feeling. I was not breathing. This was it, this was going to work. I knew it was only a matter of a few minutes before my death.

I tested the cord's tension again, letting my legs go loose once more. I could feel myself going; it was going to be quick. I staggered back up in a trancelike state, barely breathing. Then I saw my door open and a nurse came in. She looked at me, then went back out of the room – presumably to get help. I didn't want help. Just a little more time. I jumped off the ledge.

I could hear a strange choking, gurgling noise, but I didn't realise that it was me, fighting for breath. I could feel my eyes flickering and I was starting to float. Death, my friend, was so very close now.

Then I became aware that the nursing staff were trying to get me down. They were finding it difficult because I had tied the knot so tight. The next thing I remember was being on the bed with staff around me. It was all very hazy and I felt I was outside my body, which was limp and seemed unable to move.

As two nurses walked me down the stairs I could feel my neck, throat and back throbbing. I was still alive and I felt nothing, just complete numbness. Even the physical pain was a very distant feeling. I remember little of the next hour, only that a nurse called Kevin who I was vaguely aware of took me outside to get some fresh air. Presumably they thought this would be good for me, though I'm not sure why.

Kevin talked to me and I remember telling him how much I loved skiing and how the beautiful mountains and being amongst idyllic views and soft white snow and laughing children offered me some sense of freedom. That night I was told I would be on a 'special'. This is a term used for patients considered to be at serious danger to themselves and requiring twenty-four-hour supervision.

I was told that I would be sleeping in a room by the nursing station that night, just in case I needed additional assistance. I didn't want to do this, but I knew they would never let me go back to my room after I had tried to kill myself. Still feeling as if I was in a trance, and very sore, I collected my favourite white pyjamas, the small teddy I had been given by the analyst and my picture of Mum on her wedding day.

I climbed into bed in the small room next to the nurses' station, feeling as childlike and alone as I had ever felt. All I really wanted was for everything to be OK and to be with my Mum again. I wanted her to be the one who was looking after me. Her and nobody else. I knew that now. For the past ten years I had been unable to admit something so painful to myself – it was just too much to bear. But with therapy, and with time, I was now at a point where I could miss her, and long for her to be with me, even though that brought with it the ache of her loss.

I placed the photo of her beside the bed and held the teddy close to me. It was dark and Kevin, the nurse who had taken me outside, was sitting next to me in the chair by my bed. The door was ajar and I could hear the footsteps of nurses going up and down the corridor. It was noisier than the room I had been in before, because it was next to the nursing station. It wasn't easy to try to sleep with a stranger sitting in the room and with the door ajar. But leaving the door open is standard practice in hospitals when a patient is being observed one to one by a nurse, for the safety of both the patient and the nurse. But when Kevin got up and closed the door, I barely noticed. It was only when I went back over the scene afterwards that I remembered he had done this.

I wasn't in a state to notice anything. I was in shock and traumatised by my suicide attempt and my feelings of desperation about the past. As Kevin walked back to sit down I turned onto my front. I was restless and couldn't get comfortable. Kevin moved to sit beside me on the bed and began rubbing my back. It felt nice and soothing. It was so seldom that anyone touched me. I had never had the cuddles, stroking and physical warmth that so many parents give their children, and this small gesture seemed comforting.

Then he put his hand up my pyjama top and continued rubbing my back, skin to skin. This was when alarm bells went off in my head and suddenly I realised that the door was shut and I was on my own with a male nurse who was rubbing my back. I felt my body tense, my eyes widen and my jaw go rigid. I was exhausted and frightened and I didn't know how to tell Kevin to get off. I knew that he most definitely shouldn't have closed the door or be rubbing my back inside my pyjamas, but I felt powerless to stop him.

I told myself that he meant no harm – he was just comforting me after my ordeal and soon another nurse would be coming in to check on us. In fact, someone surely had to notice that the door had been shut when it was meant to be open. I could hear nurses walking past the door. They all knew what had happened in the past hour and that I was on special watch. And they knew I was in the room on my own with a male member of staff, so apart from anything else the door should have been open to protect him, as a professional staff member, from unwarranted accusations.

At this point Kevin said, 'You should have a female nurse do this for you.' I couldn't speak. I tried to make a sound to imply that yes, of course I should. I think now that he must have been testing my reactions. Would I scream? Would I sit up and say, 'How dare you?' Or would I be compliant and silent?

It is well known that any adult who has been sexually abused in childhood finds it much more difficult to respond to situations of this nature. As a child being forced into inappropriate sexual compliance, you learn not to fight, to keep silent, that you have no rights and can't escape, and that the only thing to do is to give in and bear it until the ordeal is over. All the normal and appropriate adult-child boundaries are removed, so instead of learning how to say no or protect yourself, you grow up with no concept of self-protection or rights over your own body. All your instincts are denied, and the result is that you become vulnerable to other sexual predators and abusers.

Given my background, and that I had survived a suicide attempt in the past hour, it was not surprising that I did not attempt to struggle or scream. Even if I had, I was weak and exhausted and my throat, neck and back were extremely sore.

Kevin knew all this and no doubt he counted on it.

I was unable to move as Kevin moved his hand to the side of my body, slipped his hand underneath me to my left breast, then turned me onto my back.

I froze. He must have been able to feel the tension in my body – I was as rigid as an ironing board and I kept my eyes averted from him. I felt I was no longer me and I could feel myself drifting as I prepared myself to be raped.

His behaviour was that of an experienced rapist. I knew this from the abuse I had suffered as a child. Kevin knew what he was doing; he wasn't nervous in the least. And I knew, with every instinct I had, that here was a practised predator.

Suddenly the door opened and in an instant he removed his hand and jumped back into the chair. Wow, that was quick! He really *did* know what he was doing. But, thankfully, I was now safe. A head popped around the door to ask if Kevin was OK and whether he needed a drink. He said he was fine, and as quickly as the door had opened and I had been safe, the door was shut again and I was unsafe once more.

I was terrified of being raped. I could barely cope with what had already happened in my life. Surely I didn't deserve more hurt and anguish. But it appeared that I did, and I told myself that what followed was my punishment for attempting suicide.

I stared beyond Kevin to a place he could not see, a private place of my own, as he pulled down the bed covers and took off my pyjama bottoms. I felt exposed and degraded. I was not consenting, I was not joining in. In fact I was doing everything I knew to make my unwillingness clear: I froze and made my body become as rigid as possible. There would be no disguising this level of inflexibility in my body as I knew only too well how to do it.

After Kevin had removed my pyjama bottoms I could feel his disgusting hands all over me, feeling my body. The body I had tried so hard over the years to come to terms with was being used and violated yet again. As he parted my thighs and felt my vagina I knew there was no escaping the rape.

He pulled my legs apart and raped me. His forced entry into me was painful. I gasped and shook. Despite my gasps he continued, and then after he had finished, he raped me all over again. He told me how beautiful my hair was and that I was aroused. This was just a sick self-justification for his evil actions. An attempt to pretend that this was something normal, instead of the rape of a vulnerable patient by a nurse charged with that patient's care.

Throughout my ordeal I could hear the footsteps of nursing staff passing by.

Whilst Kevin had raped the *body* of a young woman I have no doubt that on this occasion he had raped the *mind* of a child. After my suicide attempt I was in a childlike state and had regressed into my girlhood. I lay in bed in my white pyjamas, with my teddy and my photo of my Mum. All of these indicated my desperate attempt to be a child again whilst trapped in a woman's body. As a trained professional Kevin would have known just how vulnerable and helpless I was.

After he had raped me he ejaculated all over my back and then wiped his semen off me with toilet paper. Then he said, 'I've got to have a fag' and, despite the strict ban on smoking in the hospital, he sat and smoked a cigarette. To this day I hate the smell of tobacco smoke – it makes me feel sick and full of panic. I could take no more. I forced myself into a dark, dreamless sleep.

When I woke the following morning my pyjama bottoms were back on. He must have dressed me after I had passed out. There was a female nurse sitting beside me in the chair and the door was open, just as it should have been. I went over to the toilet and noticed that my pyjamas had blood on them. I hadn't realised that he had made me bleed, and I felt very sore. When I got back into bed I could see that there was blood on the sheets too. The nurse, who hadn't noticed the stains, told me that her name was Linda and asked whether I'd like any breakfast. I shook my head. My mind was racing as I tried to decide what to do. If I told the staff what Kevin had done, would they believe me? And if they did, would they panic and try to cover up what had happened?

I knew, with absolute certainty, that Kevin had raped before and would rape again if he wasn't stopped. I was afraid he would return that night and rape me again, and I was even more afraid that he would rape other very vulnerable patients. His confidence and arrogance had been breathtaking. He had got away with it before and no doubt believed that he would keep getting away with it.

I said to Linda, 'Can I tell you something that you won't tell anyone else, and will you help me do something about it?' She was very pleasant, but she said she couldn't promise not to tell. I kept repeating my request, pleading with her, and she kept saying that she couldn't make such a promise.

By lunchtime I couldn't hold out any longer – I had to have a bath. I decided I could use my pyjamas as evidence and I hid them in a plastic bag. I had learned a lot during my failed attempt to have my father prosecuted, and I knew that this evidence was vital. Then I changed the sheet on the bed for a clean one that Linda got me. She offered to help, but I said I could do it.

After that I phoned Stuart. I couldn't make a private call because there were nurses going past the phone, so I simply said to him, 'Please can I come and see you today?' He said that the soonest I could come was the next day. Had he known the truth he would have told me to come immediately, as he later confirmed. But I couldn't tell him, so I had to accept that I must wait another night.

Back in my room I thought of all the people I knew and who among them might be able to cope with hearing what had happened and help me. Annie and Chris were the obvious ones, but they were both away, as it was the summer holidays. I called a colleague of Annie's at the project where she worked, but she was on her way out and said to the woman who answered, 'Tell Gayle I'll ring her back.' So I phoned Dan, the boy I had become close friends with at secondary school.

We had stayed friends ever since, and Dan, who was now working in London, said he would come that evening. I knew that he would help me, and that I could rely on him. When he arrived I asked for some privacy and the nurse agreed to wait outside the room. Dan sat down beside me and I told him what had happened. He was horrified, and asked me what I would like him to do. I told him I would tell Stuart the next day, but in the meantime I needed to know whether Kevin was coming on duty that night. Dan went to the nursing station to check and came back to confirm that he wasn't – he was on a night off.

Dan stayed with me for a few hours that evening, and the next day I went up to Stuart's office. Ticehurst had a hospital car and they agreed to drive me to see Stuart, after I had insisted that I must see him.

When I got there I told him the whole story. He too was deeply shocked, as well as outraged that such a thing could have happened in a hospital. I went back to Ticehurst and in the meantime Stuart spoke to them and told them what had happened, but there was no suggestion of getting the police. In fact, when I asked for the police they resisted, and several of those who were told my story refused to believe me.

I insisted that the police should be called, and two officers came and took me to give a statement to a specially trained female officer in a purpose-built victim suite.

I didn't find it at all easy, going over and over the details of the rape. But I was determined to do it. This time I was not going to keep silent, I was going to stand up for myself and for all the other victims and potential victims who couldn't stand up for themselves. Most of all I felt I must stop this man raping another woman, because I was certain he would if he got the chance. This time I was going to do things my way.

Once I had given my statement, a full investigation was started and Kevin was suspended. I knew it would take some time before he was charged and prosecuted, and in the meantime I was due to start university.

My hopes of a nurturing, supportive stay at Ticehurst, and of finally talking about my mother's death, had been dashed in the cruellest way possible. But I wasn't going to let what had happened there destroy the life that I was now building for myself. I was going to go to university, no matter what.

19

University

Rather than moving into student accommodation, as I had planned, I decided to stay with the Smiths for another year. I felt safe with them: their home was familiar and besides, trying to organise somewhere to live after what I had just been through was simply too much. I had only six weeks left until my first year at university began, and I needed that time to prepare myself.

Luckily, they were very happy to have me stay on. When I had left for Ticehurst they had told me to come back afterwards and to stay as long as I liked. I was grateful for their warm support as I faced the challenges of full-time study and meeting many new people when I was still in a state of shock. I told the Smiths about the rape, and over time I also told a few close friends. Some found it hard to know what to say to me, but all were sympathetic and offered to help in any way they could.

Stuart was also a great support. He continued to be there for me, no matter what, and helped me through my bleakest moments. Along with the people who cared most – Annie, Chris, John Buss and my close friends – he encouraged me to go ahead with my plans and refuse to let what had happened at Ticehurst dictate the course of my life.

A few years earlier I might have been unable to carry on with any kind of life after such an appalling experience as that rape. But the way I had managed to take charge of the situation and fight back afterwards proved to be a turning point for me. Now I knew that I was not just a victim, that I had courage and strength and could do things for myself. So in late September 1996 I arrived on campus to begin my course and join in the wild exuberance of freshers' week.

I had been worried about whether I could concentrate on my studies, when it had always been so hard for me to do so in the past. However, I was very determined to make it work and luckily I enjoyed my chosen subject from the start, which made a real difference. I had always known that education was important and that it could only be a good decision to go to university: I found the lectures, tutorials and debates engaging and interesting. At long last I felt I was really using my brain.

From day one I made new and lasting friendships. I also got involved with the university trampoline club and was delighted when I was asked to coach the team and be president of the club. They weren't a strong team and were happy to let me go ahead and do whatever I wanted. So I set about bringing the team up to a higher standard, improving the club and expanding membership.

The trampoline club gave me a focus away from my studies. I really enjoyed my involvement with it and put in a lot of hours. And I also enjoyed becoming part of a new group of friends. But in the back of my mind I was always aware that the rape case was looming.

Kevin had been charged early on. It was about as clear-cut a case of rape as was possible, given that my pyjamas provided unequivocal evidence and that, as a patient under the hospital's care, I hadn't been in a position to consent to sex. In addition, the police discovered that Kevin had swapped shifts with another nurse so that he could look after me that night. The hospital was also at fault, in that they shouldn't have allowed a male nurse to be alone with me and shouldn't have allowed the door of my room to be shut.

Knowing that he couldn't claim that I had consented, Kevin denied that the whole thing had ever happened, and although the evidence was always going to prove him a liar he insisted on pleading not guilty. The case was due to be heard at Lewes Crown Court in the winter of 1997, over a year after the rape. To add to the already damning evidence against him the police had interviewed several former patients who confirmed that he had raped them too.

I spent many weeks preparing myself to give evidence in court. I dreaded it, but I had to do it and I would. In my mind were images of the women and girls he might rape in the future if he got off.

In the build-up to the case I had to be assessed by a psychiatrist chosen by the defence team. He believed me, and offered to give evidence for the prosecution.

We were all set to go to court when, a couple of weeks before the case was to be heard, I was told that it had been delayed. The delays continued, and the final court date wasn't set until another six months had passed.

By this time I was at the end of my second year at university. I had spent that year living with five other friends in a student house on campus. It felt really good to be with friends and peers, sharing the same life and the same transition to adulthood. While it was hard to feel happy with the rape case looming over me there were many positive changes in my life. I was eating more healthily and was better able to control any suicidal thoughts.

I also had a lot of fun working with the trampoline club, helping to bring the team up to a standard where they were able to compete nationally, and continuing to find ways to improve the club. It was a proud moment when, towards the end of my second year, I was voted the university's Sportswoman of the Year.

Perhaps most significantly of all, I took the plunge and dated a fellow student. Until then I had stayed away from romantic relationships: the whole area felt too difficult and dangerous. But I wanted to be the same as the other students, to be one of the crowd, instead of the one who was 'different'. And in order to be the same I was willing to take the risk of exploring new territory. I had been asked out before and said no, but the next time a boy I liked asked me out, I decided to give it a go.

We dated for about seven months, and although it didn't work out it was a good experience because it moved me forward and got me past the hurdle of getting involved with someone. I didn't find it easy being in a relationship, but I stuck with it until I realised that we just weren't suited. I liked him, but it wasn't love, and eventually it didn't feel right.

The relationship wasn't helped by the fact that throughout this time the trial still hung over me. When the court date was finally set and I was assured that this time it would definitely go ahead, I braced myself to do what I had to. After two years of waiting, preparing and living with what had happened, I just wanted to go into court and get through the trial so that I could try to move on.

Then, on the first day of the trial, the police phoned to tell me the news that, the night before, Kevin had taken an overdose before getting into bed next to his girlfriend. In the morning she had found him dead.

I was stunned. It was an appalling turn of events. I had wanted to see him go to prison, which was what he deserved, but I had never wanted him dead. And while I felt sorry that he had died, I also felt cheated. After the endless intrusive interviews and procedures to which I had been subjected over the previous two years in preparation for a trial, it all turned out to have been for nothing.

Kevin's death stayed with me for a long time. It was an

awful thing to have happened and was very hard to come to terms with. But, as with the rape itself, I was determined it shouldn't knock me off the path I was now set on.

A few weeks later I began the third and final year of my course. I threw myself into my dissertation, which was on women's refuges. I spent many hours reading and writing about the subject, and gaining a thorough knowledge. There were many times during this research when I thought of my mother. I don't know whether she knew about refuges, but if she had gone to one, she might have got away from my father much earlier; I couldn't help wondering how different our lives might have been.

I still felt afraid sometimes that I would turn around and see my father behind me, or find a letter from him on the doormat. But as time passed and I didn't see or hear from him, gradually my fear diminished.

I finished my degree in the summer of 1999. I had done it and I felt proud. And not only had I earned a good degree, but I had taken the decision to stay on for another year to study for a Master's Degree in Health Policy and Research, writing my dissertation on homelessness and access to health care among young people.

The degree ceremony was held in Canterbury Cathedral, a few weeks after we finished our studies. After a lot of thought I had invited my mother's parents, Gran and Grandad, to come and see me receive my degree. I still saw them from time to time, and although we weren't really close I hoped they would come and feel proud of me.

They did come for the ceremony, and I was glad that they had. We didn't have a lot of time to talk because they were in the audience and I was with the other students.

Afterwards I found them in the crowd and asked them whether they would like to come with me to join my friends and their parents for a celebratory meal. They said no, they needed to get home. I was disappointed, but I understood that perhaps it would have felt too much for them. So I saw them off and then went on my own to meet up with my friends and their families.

During the next year, while working for my Master's, I lived outside the campus with friends. And it was during this year, at a party I went to with some friends in another student house, that I met a second-year politics student called Hugh. I liked him instantly, in the same way that I had liked and felt comfortable with a small handful of others in my life, my closest friends and people such as Annie and Stuart.

That night we chatted briefly, and in the following months we gradually got to know one another. He was quite shy, and I was cautious, so we went no further than a reserved friendship. But there was something about him that I was very attracted to: I found him interesting and wanted to get to know him better. Every time I bumped into him I felt the same connection with him, but we never took it any further, although he came to my birthday party later that year.

All too soon I finished my Master's and it was time to look for a job. After four years at university I was looking forward to the next step, but it was daunting as well as exciting because I also needed a place to live.

Throughout this time I had continued to see Stuart, who supported and encouraged me. I was also still in regular contact with Annie and Chris, and with my old friends, in particular Suzie and Louise, who had gone off travelling the world for a few years instead of going to university. All these people meant a lot to me; they were the threads going back to different stages of my life. I knew that, wherever I went next, I would always stay in touch with them, as well as with some of the lovely friends I had made at university.

During my time there I had become a more outgoing person. With a lot of determination – and with Stuart's support – I had managed my studies and my life on campus. I was no longer the silent, fearful and depressed girl that I had been. It wasn't that the nightmares of the past had disappeared; they would always be with me. But I had moved forward: I was no longer someone who people had to worry about or who was unable to handle a normal life. I had made myself a life, and I was going to go on with it, no matter how hard, at times, that might still feel.

My first job was in London, working for a company gathering social statistics. Just before I started work, in January 2001, I moved into a flat in south London with a friend of mine who had done the same degree and with a couple of other friends.

The flat-share was great, but the job was awful. I hated dealing with statistics and I left after three months. I decided to do temp work for a while and joined an agency which sent me to work for the social services department of an London borough as a researcher on a project to determine residential-care strategy for children. This was, of course, a field I knew about from personal experience. It was an intensive project in which I was expected to put forward proposals, and I loved it. I liked the work, which seemed ideal for me. I was dealing with an area I knew something about, using all the skills I had acquired at university and, I hoped, doing something positive for children in the same position that I had once been in.

I had been employed on a four-month contract. At the end of the project I applied for a job as a policy researcher, based in the Cabinet Office. I was delighted when I got the job and was given a year-long contract. This new job was in Westminster, in an office close to Whitehall, and I found it fascinating being so close to the heart of government.

I liked the fact that in the jobs I did people judged me for who I was and didn't need to know all about me. It felt so different to be able to start with a blank slate and fill in as much or as little as I chose. It wasn't that I kept things secret, simply that in a work situation you don't need to know all about a person's childhood or background;

you simply need to know that they can do the job. Other bits and pieces of information will filter through, but that's not what really matters. This allowed me to be the same as everyone else, and it was a good feeling.

I did, however, want to do something to help children who were in a similar situation to the one I'd been in. Not long after leaving university I was invited to become a member of a panel of professionals assessing those who were applying to be foster-parents. The panel, which was voluntary, wanted someone who had been fostered themselves, and I fitted the bill. We sat once a month and I stayed on the panel for the next five years, always having to negotiate with new employers to allow me that one day a month off. When the project ended, I volunteered to join a new one and I plan to carry on with this voluntary work for as long as I can.

It meant – and still does mean – a lot to me to have an input into choosing foster-carers. I knew so much about what vulnerable kids needed and felt this was an area in which I could really contribute.

In the meantime my flatmate Andy had gone off travelling and the rest of us decided to move out of the flat. I moved in with a girl called Kate, a friend from university. We got on really well and over the year that we lived together we became very close. We also had an extremely active social life, going our together or with friends most evenings. After all the years I had spent feeling so alone, this closeness and the fun we had were wonderful for me.

In February that year I turned twenty-eight. A few weeks later it was Kate's birthday, and we decided to go out for a few drinks. It was also my friend Anna's birthday, so I planned to have a drink with Kate and then go on to join Anna and some other friends.

Kate told me she had agreed to meet an old friend of hers at Waterloo, so I went with her. Kate's friend was bringing someone else along, and then the four of us would go out for a few drinks.

As we stood on the platform at Waterloo, Kate spotted her friend. I turned around and, to my great surprise, saw Hugh coming up the platform with Kate's friend. He was her 'someone else'. Hugh was as surprised as I was; we'd lost touch after I had left Kent two years earlier. But although I hadn't been friendly enough with him to swap details when we left, he had made a deep impression on me and I had never stopped thinking about him. When I graduated with my Master's degree, knowing that Hugh would be finishing his degree at the same time I had looked at the lists of graduates to see whether he had got a First and the politics prize – he had, and I was so pleased for him. Now, seeing him again so unexpectedly, I felt so happy – and also bowled over by how gorgeous he was. 'Do you two know each other?' Kate asked, as Hugh and I, both a little tongue-tied, said hello.

We went out for out drink and, loath to leave Hugh, I persuaded Anna's party to join us and we all spent the evening together. Hugh and I chatted for most of that night, catching up on our lives since we had last met. He was living in London and was also involved in political research, so we had a lot to talk about.

I went home knowing that this time we would not lose touch; we had swapped numbers and met a day or two later. From that meeting our relationship took off. Neither of us had any expectations, or put any pressure on the other – we simply enjoyed being together and grew naturally closer and fonder of one another.

Four months later, one day in July, Kate announced that she was going to do a Master's degree at London University's School of Oriental and African Studies and would no longer be able to afford the flat. Once again I needed somewhere to live. That night I was out with Hugh and I told him I had to move. 'You can move into my spare room, if you want,' he told me. The next day I phoned him and said, 'Did you mean it?' He'd been a bit drunk when he'd said it, so I'm not sure he remembered it all that clearly. But he very sweetly said, 'Of course' and shortly afterwards I moved all my things into his London house.

It all felt very easy and natural, and it worked for both of us. From then on Hugh and I were very much together, and I was very happy living with him. We got on well, seldom if ever argued, and enjoyed one another's company enormously.

I told Hugh all about my background a little at a time. He knew one or two things from our time at university, and I filled in the rest when I felt ready. He never pushed me and his attitude to everything I told him was very laid-back and non-judgemental. He didn't get stirred up or overdo the sympathy, he just accepted it all and, most importantly, it made no difference at all to the way he felt about me. He never treated me with kid gloves or questioned me, and this convinced me that he really did care about me for myself, and not because he felt sorry for me.

Hugh's love and total acceptance were like healing balm to my soul. If he could love me, knowing all there was to know about me, then perhaps I really was lovable after all. It wasn't that the nightmares of the past suddenly evaporated: they were still with me, and always would be. But they became less important; there was a shift in me, so that my life became about what was happening in the moment, not about what had happened in the past. And more than anything else that freed me to stop simply existing and really *live*.

20

Love and a new life

After I moved to London, Gran gave me the phone number of my cousin James, the son of my Aunt Jane, and told me he had been asking about me. I had always liked James and was pleased to hear that he wanted to get in touch, so I rang him and we met and caught up on our lives. He knew very little of what had happened to me in the years since we'd been children together, and I didn't feel the need to tell him all about it. It was just nice to see him, and we agreed to keep in regular contact.

By this time I had very little contact with anyone else from my family, so seeing James, and his promise to keep in touch, meant a lot to me. I had tried over the years to maintain a connection with family members, but it seemed that they simply didn't want to reciprocate. For a long time I had sent Christmas and birthday cards to my brother, sister, aunt, uncle and cousins through my Gran and Grandad, but I hardly ever received any in return and in the end I gave up, though the hurt of their rejection was very hard.

Even my grandparents became increasingly distant. For the past few years it had always been me who got in touch with them, but it seemed to me that they were more and more reluctant to respond, so I contacted them less and less.

I didn't understand why this should be. All the rest of the family were in contact with one another, but none of them wanted to know me. Was it because somehow they all blamed me for my mother's death? I couldn't help feeling that it must be so – I could find no other explanation.

I still blamed myself, too. With Stuart's help, and Hugh's love, I had come to terms with a great deal. I no longer felt actively suicidal: I had a great deal to live for, and I valued immensely the life I had achieved. But I also knew that the nightmares would never completely disappear, and the guilt I felt over my mother's death was reinforced by my family's continuing rejection of me.

My friends were the closest I had to a family, and I put a lot of effort into keeping in touch with them, regularly seeing all the people who had given me friendship and support over the years. Louise came back from her travels around the world and moved into a flat not far from me, and we began seeing one another often, our friendship as solid as ever. In September 2006 she gave birth to a beautiful little girl, Ella. Kate married, and I read at her wedding. Dan, who had also married, lived not far from me and we often got together, and Suzie was now the mother of two gorgeous children.

I had not heard from my father for some years, though

I still looked over my shoulder from time to time. I had heard, through Gran, that he was now divorced from his second wife and had been turned out of the Church for cheating on his thesis. A small article in a national paper pointed out that the Church had accepted the fact that he'd killed his wife, but had drawn the line at his cheating on coursework. I had to smile. I had no idea what he had done next, and no interest in knowing. He was part of the past.

Meanwhile my work was going from strength to strength. From my Cabinet Office job I moved on to work for the child-protection department of another London borough's social services department. I found the work challenging and hard. It was distressing to see families with enormous difficulties and problems, not because it reminded me of my own background – these families were in very different circumstances – but because they were going through such tough times. Ultimately I felt that this kind of work was not for me and although I learned a great deal in this job I decided to move on to something more analytical.

After a year and a half I moved on to another borough, this time working in the field of domestic violence. This was a strategic role, overseeing the way in which the voluntary and statutory services in the borough – such as the police, social services, victim support and so on – addressed domestic violence. I spent my time analysing their roles and supporting them in working together and complementing one another's activities.

I enjoyed this job far more, and stayed for two years until I was offered a job focusing on children and domestic violence. This involved working with teachers, heads of schools, governors and children in a borough in London. The idea was to educate the children to become healthy adults who respected one another and were not violent to one another, and who would not put up with violence.

This, of course, was a subject close to my heart. I couldn't undo what had happened to my mother. But perhaps I could help to ensure that today's children would not be afraid to report violence at home, and would become adults who would be able to avoid, or help themselves out of, violent relationships.

Shortly before I began this job, in July 2006, Hugh had asked me to marry him. I had no doubts. This gentle, intelligent and loving man was the one with whom I wanted to spend the rest of my life. I knew that Hugh loved me, not for what I had been through or because he felt he had to rescue me from my past but for who I was now.

We decided to marry six months later, on 6 January 2007. We chose that time because the Christmas period had always been so grim for me, and I wanted to change that. Coming so soon after my mother's death, and immediately after her funeral, Christmas had always been a very difficult time to get though. And I had spent so many Christmases wishing that my family circumstances had been different.

Now I could choose to make Christmas a time of excitement and anticipation, and the New Year a time of hope and optimism.

Hugh's family, his mother, father and sister, were exceptionally warm, open and welcoming people. I had got to know them over the years and they had always made me feel welcome. When we told them we were going to marry they offered to help in every way. With their generosity and support we planned the wedding just as we both wanted it, down to the last detail.

The date arrived far more quickly than I had expected. I had only started my new job a couple of months before, and had spent the run-up to Christmas juggling work and wedding preparations.

Hugh's sister Emma had helped me find the dress at Suzanne Neville, the designer in Knightsbridge. It was just what I wanted: a sleek and elegant ivory dress, off the shoulder, with a fitted bodice, a gently flared skirt and a small train. When I put it on, Emma and I both said, 'This is the one.' I hoped that Hugh would like it as much as I did and, when he eventually saw it, he did.

I had asked two close friends to make speeches. The first was Louise, as my oldest friend and the one person among my friends who had known my mother. I couldn't think of anybody better to speak about me. The second was Agnes, a close friend from university.

The night before the wedding Louise rang me to say that she had written the speech but needed to know whether it would be all right to mention my Mum. She wasn't sure whether this would be what I wanted. We both burst into tears and I said I would text her later, because I couldn't talk about it.

I had decided, some months before, that on our wedding day I would only have positive thoughts and memories of my Mum. After I put down the phone I asked Hugh what he thought I should say to Louise. He said he thought it would be really nice for her to mention Mum. So I sent Louise a text saying that I would love her to go ahead and say whatever she thought best.

Hugh and I had decided to forget about tradition and spend the night before the wedding together. I wanted to begin my wedding day by waking up beside the man with whom I was going to spend the rest of my life.

The wedding was to be at five p.m., the latest time allowed under UK law. This gave us the whole day in which to prepare and gave plenty of time to those guests who had a long way to travel.

I woke early, nervous with excitement and confident that our day would be perfect. Part of me couldn't quite believe that not only was I getting married, but it was to this wonderful man. It seemed a lifetime away when I was so unhappy and had believed there was no future for me. Now I had everything to live for, and someone to share it all with.

Far too excited to sleep any more, I left Hugh still fast asleep in bed, hopped on our Vespa and went to the supermarket to get some food. I returned an hour later to find Hugh still sleeping!

A little while later, as Hugh left to go to his parents' house to get ready, the bridesmaids arrived. We had asked Charlotte, Ellie and Rosie, the three daughters of Joanne and Neil White, my friends from the time before I went to university, when I had lived with the Smiths. We had remained good friends and, having known them since they were babies, I loved all three girls very much. From Hugh's side we asked his cousin's daughter, Laura. She was to meet us at the register office, while Charlotte, Ellie and Rosie would get ready with me.

As soon as they had arrived all four of us went together to the local hairdresser, five minutes from the house. I had invited a few close friends to help me get ready and calm my nerves and when we got back they were beginning to arrive. Louise's older sister Rachel did my make-up, while Louise and Kate opened the champagne and handed me a glass. Agnes paced up and down rehearsing her speech, clearly very nervous!

They all helped me into my dress, the flowers arrived and we waited for Hugh's father to collect us. As he arrived and the bridesmaids stood ready, looking adorable, I thought this is it – this is our day, our wedding and the beginning of a wonderful future. I had spent so much of my life surviving, and fighting for what I wanted. Now the day had arrived when I could put everything behind me and I was filled with a feeling that was both powerful and positive.

As we sat in the car I thought about Hugh. We had only been apart for a few hours, but I totally adored him and couldn't wait to see him again. I knew that his kind eyes and warm smile would calm my nerves. A little while later, as I walked up the aisle, my arm tucked under Hugh's father's, the four bridesmaids following us and Hugh waiting for me, I felt like the luckiest woman alive.

The service was short, though special for us. Hugh's cousin sang and we had two close friends read, one of them from university days, the other being Chloe Smith, the daughter of the family who had offered me a home for three years before I began university. Afterwards we walked out together hand in hand to the steps of the Town Hall, where we were showered with confetti.

At the reception I was able, at last, to greet all our guests. I had hoped that my grandparents might come, as representatives of my family. But, to my great disappointment, they decided that they could not. I never really understood why, but wondered if, as the only family members on my side, they might have felt awkward. I was very sad about this and felt strongly that they should have been there for their daughter, my mother.

However, my cousin James did come, with his wife. He had married a year or two earlier and I was so pleased to see him there.

Most importantly, the people who had been my greatest allies and supporters over the years had come. I saw Annie and Chris, my two staunch and loyal friends, with their children, along with John Buss, the GP who had given me so much support – all three adults smiling at me with such pride and pleasure. Dan and his wife were there, too. Then there were the Smiths, Mike, Penny, Jake and Chloe, along with the bridesmaids' parents, Joanne and Neil White. All my old school and university friends and those I had met since were there. And then there was my old school friend Suzie. And, of course, Louise.

The evening went by so quickly. Every moment was special; Hugh and I danced, cut our cake, talked to our guests and enjoyed a wonderful meal. It felt so good to be surrounded by people I cared about and who cared about me. Many of Hugh's relatives came up to welcome me to the family, and that touched me deeply. His mother, father and sister had always been so welcoming and now his aunts, uncles and cousins were making me feel even more a part of my new family.

Towards the end of the meal came the speeches. Hugh's father spoke warmly, welcoming everyone to the wedding. Hugh and I had decided to make a speech together, and we took turns to thank everyone involved for all they had done. Agnes spoke about university and our friendship. All the speeches were special, but Louise's was the most special of all. She talked about us playing, as little girls, and then made her tender and sensitive reference to how much I missed Mum and would have loved her to be there.

She got it just right. I did miss Mum. I always will. I miss what we did have, and I miss what we didn't: the relationship I would love to have had with her, if things had been different for us.

But as Hugh and I set off for our honeymoon, with waves and cheers and endless hugs and good wishes from our friends and family, I knew that achieving the happiness I now had was the very best tribute I could ever have given Mum. I'm sure it's what she would have wanted.